Fremdsprachentexte

Ten British Women Writers

Contemporary Short Stories

Herausgegeben von
Barbara Puschmann-Nalenz

Philipp Reclam jun. Stuttgart

Diese Ausgabe darf nur in der Bundesrepublik Deutschland, in Österreich und in der Schweiz vertrieben werden.

Universal-Bibliothek Nr. 9077

Gesamtherstellung: Reclam, Ditzingen. Printed in Germany 2000

ISBN 3-15-009077-6

Inhalt

Susan Hill

The Badness Within Him

The night before, he had knelt beside his bed and prayed for a storm, an urgent, hysterical prayer. But even while he prayed he had known that there could be no answer, because of the badness within him, a badness which was living and growing like a cancer. So that he was not surprised to draw back the curtains and see the pale, glittering mist of another hot day. But he was angry. He did not want the sun and the endless stillness and brightness, the hard-edged shadows and the steely gleam of the sea. They came to this place every summer, they had been here, now, since the first of August, and they had one week more left. The sun had shone from the beginning. He wondered how he would bear it.

At the breakfast table, Jess sat opposite to him and her hand kept moving up to rub at the sunburned skin which was peeling off her nose.

"Stop *doing* that."

Jess looked up slowly. This year, for the first time, Col felt the difference in age between them, he saw that Jess was changing, moving away from him to join the adults. She was almost fourteen.

9 **to glitter:** glitzern, flimmern.
12 **gleam:** Glanz, Schimmer.

"What if the skin doesn't grow again? What then? You look awful enough now."

She did not reply, only considered him for a long time, before returning her attention to the cereal plate. After a moment, her hand went up again to the peeling skin.

Col thought, I hate it here. I hate it. I *hate* it. And he clenched his fist under cover of the table until the fingernails hurt him, digging into his palm. He had suddenly come to hate it, and the emotion frightened him. It was the reason why he had prayed for the storm, to break the pattern of long, hot, still days and waken the others out of their contentment, to change things. Now, everything was as it had always been in the past and he did not want the past, he wanted the future.

But the others were happy here, they slipped into the gentle, lazy routine of summer as their feet slipped into sandals, they never grew bored or angry or irritable, never quarrelled with one another. For days now Col had wanted to quarrel.

How had he ever been able to bear it? And he cast about, in his frustration, for some terrible event, as he felt the misery welling up inside him at the beginning of another day.

I hate it here. He hated the house itself, the chintz cur-

8 **to clench one's fist:** die Faust ballen.
13 **contentment:** Zufriedenheit.
24 **to well up:** aufwallen, -steigen (Gefühl).
26 **chintz:** Chintz (bunt bedrucktes Gewebe mit glatter, glänzender Oberfläche).

tains and covers bleached by the glare of the sun, and the crunch of sand like sugar spilled in the hall and along the tiled passages, the windows with peeling paint always open on to the garden, and the porch cluttered with sandshoes and buckets and deckchairs, the muddle and shabbiness of it all.

They all came down to breakfast at different times, and ate slowly and talked of nothing, made no plans, for that was what the holiday was for, a respite from plans and time-tables.

Fay pulled out the high chair and sat her baby down next to Col.

"You can help him with his egg."

"Do I have to?"

Fay stared at him, shocked that anyone should not find her child desirable.

"Do help, Col, you know the baby can't manage by himself."

"Col's got a black dog on his shoulder."

"Shut up."

"A perfectly enormous, coal black, monster of a dog!"

1 **to bleach:** bleichen.
glare: grelles Licht.
2 **crunch:** Knirschen.
to spill: verschütten.
3 **tiled:** gefliest.
4 **porch:** Veranda.
4 f. **cluttered:** vollgestellt, -gestopft; übersät.
5 **sandshoes:** Strandschuhe.
deckchair: Liegestuhl.
6 **muddle:** Durcheinander, Unordnung.
9 **respite:** (Ruhe-)Pause, Erholung.

He kicked out viciously at his sister under the table. Jess began to cry.

"Now, Col, you are to apologise please." His mother looked paler than ever, exhausted. Fay's baby dug fingers of toast down deeper and deeper into the yolk of egg.

"You hurt me, you hurt me."

He looked out of the window. The sea was a thin, glistening line. Nothing moved. Today would be the same as yesterday and all the other days – nothing would happen, nothing would change. He felt himself itching beneath his skin.

They had first come here when he was three years old. He remembered how great the distance had seemed as he jumped from rock to rock on the beach, how he had scarcely been able to stretch his leg across and balance. Then, he had stood for minute after minute feeling the damp ribs of sand under his feet. He had been enchanted with everything. He and Jess had collected buckets full of sea creatures from the rock pools and put them into a glass aquarium in the scullery, though always the starfish and anemones and limpets died after a few, captive days. They had taken jam jars up on

4 f. **fingers of toast** (pl.): Toaststreifen.
5 **yolk:** Eigelb.
8 f. **to glisten:** glänzen, glitzern.
18 **rib:** Rippe, Rille.
18 f. **to be enchanted with s.th.:** von etwas begeistert, bezaubert, entzückt sein.
21 **scullery:** Spülküche.
22 **starfish:** Seestern.
limpet: Napfschnecke.
23 **captive:** in Gefangenschaft.

to West Cliff and walked along, at the hottest part of the day, looking for chrysalis on the grass stalks. The salt had dried in white tide marks around their brown legs, and Col had reached down and rubbed some off with his finger and then licked it. In the sun lounge the moths and butterflies had swollen and cracked open their frail, papery coverings and crept out like babies from the womb, and he and Jess had sat up half the night by the light of moon or candle, watching them. And so it had been every year and often, in winter or windy spring in London, he remembered it all, the smell of the sunlit house and the feeling of the warm sea lapping against his thighs and the line of damp woollen bathing shorts outside the open back door. It was another world, but it was still there, and when every summer came they would return to it, things would be the same.

Yet now, he wanted to do some violence in this house, he wanted an end to everything. He was afraid of himself.

"Col's got a black dog on his shoulder!"

So he left them and went for a walk on his own, over the track beside the gorse bushes and up on to the coarse grass of the sheep field behind West Cliff. The

2 **chrysalis:** Insektenpuppe.
grass stalk: Grashalm.
5 **sun lounge** (auch: *sun parlour*): Glasveranda.
7 **frail:** zerbrechlich.
8 **womb:** Mutterleib.
13 **to lap:** plätschern.
thigh: Oberschenkel.
23 **gorse:** Stechginster.

mist was rolling away, the sea was white-gold at the edges, creaming back. On the far side of the field there were poppies.

He lay down and pressed his face and hands into the warm turf until he could smell the soil beneath and gradually, he felt the warmth of the sun on his back and it soothed him.

In the house, his mother and sisters left the breakfast table and wandered upstairs to find towels and sunhats and books, content that this day should be the same as all the other days, wanting the summer to last. And later, his father would join them for the weekend, coming down on the train from London, he would discard the blue city suit and emerge, hairy and thickly fleshed, to lie on a rug and snore and play with Fay's baby, rounding off the family circle.

By eleven it was hotter than it had been all summer, the dust rose in soft clouds when a car passed down the lane to the village, and did not settle again, and the leaves of the hedges were mottled and dark, the birds went quiet. Col felt his own anger like a pain tightening around his head. He went up to the house and lay on his bed trying to read, but the room was airless and the sunlight fell in a straight, hard beam across his bed and on to the printed page, making his eyes hurt.

3 **poppy:** Klatschmohn.
5 **turf:** Grasboden.
7 **to soothe:** beruhigen.
13 **to discard:** (Kleidung) ablegen.
15 **to snore:** schnarchen.
20 **mottled:** gesprenkelt, fleckig.
21 **to tighten:** sich spannen.

When he was younger he had liked this room, he had sometimes dreamed of it when he was in London. He had collected shells and small pebbles and laid them out in careful piles, and hung up a bladder-wrack on a nail by the open window, had brought books from home about fossils and shipwrecks and propped them on top of the painted wooden chest. But now it felt too small, it stifled him, it was a childish room, a pale, dead room in which nothing ever happened and nothing would change.

After a while he heard his father's taxi come up the drive.

"Col, do watch what you're doing near the baby, you'll get sand in his eyes."

"Col, if you want to play this game with us, do, but otherwise go away, if you can't keep still, you're just spoiling it."

"Col, why don't you build a sandcastle or something?"

He stood looking down at them all, at his mother and Fay playing cards in the shade of the green parasol, and his father lying on his back, his bare, black-haired chest shiny with oil and his nostrils flaring in and out as he

3 **pebble:** Kieselstein.
4 **bladder-wrack:** Blasentang.
6 **fossil:** Fossil, Versteinerung.
to prop: lehnen.
8 **to stifle:** ersticken.
21 **parasol:** Sonnenschirm.
23 **nostril:** Nasenloch.
to flare: sich blähen.

breathed, at Jess, who had begun to build the sandcastle for the baby, instead of him. She had her hair tied back in bunches and the freckles had come out even more thickly across her cheekbones, she might have been eleven years old. But she was almost fourteen, she had gone away from him.

"Col, don't kick the sand like that, it's flying everywhere. Why don't you go and have a swim? Why can't you find something to do? I do so dislike you just hovering over us like that."

Jess had filled a small bucket with water from the rock pool, and now she bent down and began to pour it carefully into the moat. It splashed on to her bare feet and she wriggled her toes. Fay's baby bounced up and down with interest and pleasure in the stream of water and the crenellated golden castle.

Col kicked again more forcefully. The clods of sand hit the tower of the castle sideways, and, as it fell, crumbled the edges off the other towers and broke open the surrounding wall, so that everything toppled into the moat, clouding the water.

Jess got to her feet, scarlet in the face, ready to hit out at him.

3 **freckles:** Sommersprossen.
9 f. **to hover over s.o.:** um jdn. herumschleichen, -streifen.
13 **moat:** Wassergraben.
14 **to wriggle ones's toes:** mit den Zehen wackeln.
to bounce up and down: auf und nieder hüpfen, wippen.
16 **crenallated:** mit Zinnen versehen.
17 **clod:** Klumpen.
18 f. **to crumble:** abbröckeln lassen, zerkrümeln.
20 **to topple:** (ein)stürzen.
22 **scarlet:** hochrot.

"I hate you. *I hate you.*"

"Jess …"

"He wants to spoil everything, look at him, he doesn't want anyone else to enjoy themselves, he just wants to sulk and … I hate him."

Col thought, I am filled with evil, there is no hope for me. For he felt himself completely taken over by the badness within him.

"*I hate you.*"

He turned away from his sister's wild face and her mouth which opened and shut over and over again to shout her rejection of him, turned away from them all and began to walk towards the caves at the far side of the cove. Above them were the cliffs.

Three-quarters of the way up there was a ledge around which the gannets and kittiwakes nested. He had never climbed up as high as this before. There were tussocks of grass, dried and bleached bone-pale by the sea winds, and he clung on to them and to the bumps of chalky rock. Flowers grew, pale wild scabious and cliff buttercups, and when he rested, he touched his face to

5 **to sulk:** schmollen, eingeschnappt sein.
12 **rejection:** Ablehnung.
14 **cove:** (kleine) Bucht.
15 **ledge:** Sims, Vorsprung.
16 **gannet:** Tölpel (Vogelart).
kittiwake: Dreizehenmöwe.
17 **tussock:** (Gras-)Büschel.
19 **bump:** Brocken.
20 **chalky:** Kalk-.
scabious: Skabiose (Pflanzenart).
21 **buttercup:** Butterblume.

them. Above his head, the sky was enamel blue. The sea birds watched him with eyes like beads. As he climbed higher, the wash of the sea and the voices of those on the beach receded. When he reached the ledge, he got his breath and then sat down cautiously, legs dangling over the edge. There was just enough room for him. The surface of the cliff was hot on his back. He was not at all afraid.

His family were like insects down on the sand, little shapes of colour dotted about at random. Jess was a pink shape, the parasol was bottle-glass green, Fay and Fay's baby were yellow. For most of the time they were still, but once they all clustered around the parasol to look at something and then broke away again, so that it was like a dance. The other people on the beach were quite separate, each family kept itself to itself. Out beyond the curve of the cliff the beach lay like a ribbon bounded by the tide, which did not reach as far as the cove except in the storms of winter. They had never been here during the winter.

When Col opened his eyes again his head swam for a moment. Everything was the same. The sky was thin and clear. The sun shone. If he had gone to sleep he

1 **enamel blue:** emailblau.
2 **bead:** (Glas-)Perle.
3 **wash:** Wellenbewegung, Brandung.
4 **to recede:** (in der Ferne) verschwinden.
6 **to dangle:** baumeln.
10 (*to be*) **dotted about:** hingetupft, (einzeln) verstreut sein.
13 **to cluster:** sich drängen.
18 **to bound:** begrenzen, säumen.

might have tipped over and fallen forwards. The thought did not frighten him.

But all was not the same, for now he saw his father had left the family group and was padding down towards the sea. The black hairs curled up the backs of his legs and the soles of his feet were brownish pink as they turned up one after the other.

Col said, do I like my father? And thought about it. And did not know.

Fay's baby was crawling after him, its lemon-coloured behind stuck up in the air.

Now, Col half-closed his eyes, so that air and sea and sand shimmered, merging together.

Now, he felt rested, no longer angry, he felt above it all.

Now, he opened his eyes again and saw his father striding into the water, until it reached up to his chest: then he flopped onto his belly and floated for a moment, before beginning to swim.

Col thought, perhaps I am ill and *that* is the badness within me.

But if he had changed, the others had changed too. Since Fay had married and had the baby and gone to live in Berkshire, she was different, she fussed more, was concerned with the details of things, she

1 **to tip over:** umkippen.
4 **to pad:** patschen, trotten.
6 **sole:** (Fuß-)Sohle.
11 **behind:** Popo, Hinterteil.
13 **to merge together:** ineinander verschwimmen, übergehen.
18 **to flop:** sich fallen, gleiten lassen, plumpsen, platschen.

spoke to them all a trifle impatiently. And his mother was so languid. And Jess – Jess did not want his company.

Now he saw his father's dark head bobbing up and down quite a long way out to sea, but as he watched, sitting on the high cliff ledge in the sun, the bobbing stopped – began again – an arm came up and waved, though as if it were uncertain of its direction.

Col waved back.

The sun was burning the top of his head.

Fay and Fay's baby and Jess had moved in around the parasol again, their heads were bent together. Col thought, we will never be the same with one another, the ties of blood make no difference, we are separate people now. And then he felt afraid of such truth. Father's waving stopped abruptly, he bobbed and disappeared, bobbed up again.

The sea was still as glass.

Col saw that his father was drowning.

In the end, a man from the other side of the beach went running down to the water's edge and another to where the family were grouped around the parasol. Col looked at the cliff, falling away at his feet. He closed his eyes and turned around slowly and then got down on his hands and knees and began to feel for a foothold,

1 **a trifle:** ein wenig.
impatiently (adv.): ungeduldig.
2 **languid:** träge, gleichgültig.
4 f. **to bob up and down:** sich auf und nieder bewegen, (auf den Wellen) tanzen.

though not daring to look. His head was hot and throbbing.

By the time he reached the bottom, they were bringing his father's body. Col stood in the shadow of the cliff and shivered and smelled the dank, cave smell behind him. His mother and Fay and Jess stood in a line, very erect, like Royalty at the cenotaph, and in Fay's arms the baby was still as a doll.

Everyone else kept away, though Col could see that they made half-gestures, raised an arm or turned a head, occasionally took an uncertain step forward, before retreating again.

Eventually he wondered if they had forgotten about him. The men dripped water off their arms and shoulders as they walked and the sea ran off the body, too, in a thin, steady stream.

Nobody spoke to him about the cliff climb. People only spoke of baths and hot drinks and telephone messages, scarcely looking at one another as they did so, and the house was full of strangers moving from room to room.

In bed, he lay stiffly under the tight sheets and looked towards the window where the moon shone. He thought, it is my fault. I prayed for some terrible happening and the badness within me made it come about. I am punished. For this was a change greater than any he could have imagined.

1 f. **to throb:** pochen, hämmern.
5 **to shiver:** zittern.
dank: feucht, dumpfig.
7 **Royalty:** Mitglieder des Königshauses.
cenotaph: Gefallenendenkmal (in London).

When he slept he dreamed of drowning, and woke early, just at dawn. Outside the window, a dove grey mist muffled everything. He felt the cold linoleum under his feet and the dampness in his nostrils. When he reached the bottom of the stairs he saw at once that the door of the sun parlour was closed. He stood for a moment outside, listening to the creaking of the house, imagining all of them in their beds, his mother lying alone. He was afraid. He turned the brass doorknob and went slowly in.

There were windows on three sides of the room, long and uncurtained, with a view of the sea, but now there was only the fog pressing up against the panes, the curious stillness. The floor was polished and partly covered with rush matting and in the ruts of this the sand of all the summer past had gathered and lay, soft and gritty, the room smelled of seaweed. On the walls, the sepia photographs of his great-grandfather the Captain, and his naval friends and their ships. He had always liked this room. When he was small, he had sat here with his mother on warm, August evenings, drinking his mug of milk, and the smell of stocks came in to them from the

2 **dove grey:** taubenblau, blaugrau.
3 **to muffle:** (Geräusch) dämpfen.
7 **creaking:** Knarren.
13 **pane:** Fensterscheibe.
15 **rush matting:** Stroh-, Schilfmatte(n).
rut: Rille.
16 **gritty:** knirschend.
17 **seaweed:** Tang.
sepia: sepiabraun (Foto).
22 **stock:** Levkoje (Gartenblume).

open windows. The deckchairs had always been in a row outside on the terrace, empty at the end of the day. He stepped forward.

They had put his father's body on the trestle table, dressed in a shirt and covered with a sheet and a rug. His head was bare and lay on a cushion, and the hands, with the black hair over their backs, were folded together. Now, he was not afraid. His father's skin was oddly pale and shiny. He stared, trying to feel some sense of loss and sorrow. He had watched his father drown, though for a long time he had not believed it, the water had been so entirely calm. Later, he had heard them talking of a heart attack, and then he had understood better why this strong barrel of a man, down that day from the City, should have been so suddenly sinking, sinking.

The fog horn sounded outside. Then, he knew that the change had come, knew that the long, hot summer was at an end, and that his childhood had ended too, that they would never come to this house again. He knew, finally, the power of the badness within him and because of that, standing close to his father's body, he wept.

4 **trestle table:** Tapeziertisch, Tischplatte auf Böcken.

Emma Tennant

Philomela

Before I married, when we lived in Athens, the bright emptiness of the long days was made bearable by my sister Philomela, who spoke the thoughts I hardly knew I had.

Why permit yourself to be taken off like a slave? We can leave Athens and go and live in the mountains. We will be free. And if we die, anything better than the life that lies ahead of us.

I knew she was right, but I couldn't find the courage to go. The nights are cold in the mountains, and we would almost certainly perish. Tereus came and married me and we went to Thrace in a procession of such magnificence that I knew I would never come back. When my son Itylus was born, I felt as if I had been buried in a soft tomb.

I'll come and live with you, Philomela said. You won't have to wait long.

2 **Philomela:** in der griechischen Mythologie Tochter des Pandion, König von Athen, und Schwester der Prokne, Gemahlin des thrakischen Königs Tereus, dem Prokne den Sohn Itylos gebar.

13 **to perish:** zugrunde gehen, sterben.

14 **Thrace:** Thrakien, Thrazien (historische griechische Provinz).

14 f. **magnificence:** Glanz, Pomp.

17 **tomb:** Grab; Grabmal.

She never came. I moped, like the birds my children bring back when they go out for a walk. Tereus noticed, but he didn't care. The palace, as it is now, was always full of young men singing, and preparations for war, and the bustle of sandalled feet going aimlessly back and forth on the worn marble. I stayed on my couch, almost pleased that my beauty was going and that I was unable to sleep at night. It was a slow death, but no one who is buried alive dies quickly.

Then one day Tereus said he would go and find my sister. There had been no wars for two years, and the festivities were palling. He was looking older himself; perhaps only bloodshed kept him young; at any rate he wanted to travel, and he liked the idea of doing something gallant and slightly ridiculous. To his delight, everyone laughed when he said he was going to rescue my sister from her monotonous life in Athens.

It was at the height of summer that he set off. When he had gone I went down into the gardens for the first time for years and looked in an interested way at the flowers and the strolling peacocks. My children even smiled at me when I went up to them. I pretended to myself that my health had changed, that I had been ill for a long time and was now quite naturally better, but

1 **to mope:** Trübsal blasen, niedergeschlagen sein.
5 **bustle:** Geschäftigkeit, Hast.
aimlessly (adv.): ziellos.
12 **to pall:** langweilig, schal werden, an Reiz verlieren.
13 **bloodshed:** Blutvergießen.
15 **gallant: 1.** tapfer; **2.** galant.
21 **to stroll:** (umher)schlendern, -spazieren.
peacock: Pfau.

I knew that it was really because Philomela was coming that I saw these things in a different way. Her face and her voice kept flowing through me as I paced out the rest of the day, glancing foolishly at the position of the sun in the sky. It was a long journey, and it might be weeks before Tereus brought her back.

Tereus came back one winter day. The air was clear and I could see a huddle of people galloping across the plain. My throat ached, as if I had tried to shout to them across that distance, and my hands kept flying to my neck and pulling at the gold chains I wore. Then I felt I was going to cry, and I sent for Coda to bring me a herb drink that soothes my mind. I even thought for a moment of climbing to the temple. But I restrained myself, in case Philomela should climb the wide steps when I wasn't there to see her. And I wanted to show her the garden we had made, to take her into the house of which I felt suddenly proud.

Tereus' head seemed larger, I remember that. And the young men with him hung back, which they don't usually do – no one ran past me with a quick salute on the way to the courtyard and the refreshing wine. Tereus' head loomed over me like a round polished shield. His tongue moved thickly in his dry lips.

Philomela is dead, he said.

8 **huddle:** dicht gedrängte Gruppe, dichtes Knäuel, Gewirr.
13 **herb:** Kräuter-.
to soothe: beruhigen, besänftigen.
20 **to hang back:** zurückbleiben.
22 **courtyard:** Hof.
23 **to loom:** sich (drohend) abzeichnen, (auf)ragen.
shield: (Waffen-)Schild.

I spent a year in that room. When the sun lurked in the courtyard, beyond the hangings, which it did in the morning early when the slaves were washing the stone-fruited floors, I lifted my goblet of wine and poured it down my throat. All day long I called for more wine – and Coda and Dita brought it with lowered eyes.

I gave birth to another child. Itylus came and sat with me sometimes, but he was learning to go out with his father more. He had a horse of his own. When I asked him about the garden we had made, he was embarrassed and changed the subject. I began to suspect that it was overgrown, or that Tereus had got rid of it altogether. Not that I really cared. The garden had been for Philomela, and she would never come now.

When the new child was beginning to learn how to crawl about on the soft rugs in my room, I got up for the first time and went onto the wide porch that looks over the plain. It was summer, and birds were singing in the thicket of olives. My eyes were tired from crying: they had changed their shape now and slanted down in the corners instead of being round.

I gazed out at all the empty expanses around me. Sky.

1 **to lurk:** lauern, sich stehlen.
2 **hangings** (pl.): Behang; Vorhang.
3 f. **stone-fruited floor:** Steinfußboden mit Fruchtornamentik.
4 **goblet:** Becher.
18 **porch:** Veranda.
20 **thicket:** Dickicht.
21 **to slant down:** schräg nach unten hängen.
23 **to gaze:** blicken, starren.
expanse: weiter Raum, weite Fläche.

Earth. Distant mountain. None of them contained anything at all.

I leant back against a pillar and sighed. My back was weak after so long in my room. A slave came up the steps towards me. He stopped, surprised to see me there, and then prostrated himself.

He had something for me: it seemed to be a bundle of cloth. I took it listlessly – a present no doubt from one of the noble women I no longer consented to see. The slave glanced anxiously at me once, and then ran into the house. I opened the bundle, yawning.

A tapestry. My eyes were blurred, and I had to bring it up close to my face to see what scenes were depicted. Chariots in Thrace, I thought at first, and noble warriors under a spiky sun. Then I saw that the chief figure was Tereus himself.

This is amusing, I said aloud. Is Tereus worth this? I looked closer.

In the first scene, Tereus was embracing a woman passionately. Her face was obscured; I smiled. In the second, I saw it. The owner of the face was cringing at Te-

6 **to prostrate o.s.:** sich niederwerfen.
8 **listlessly** (adv.): lustlos.
9 **to consent:** zustimmen, einwilligen.
12 **tapestry:** Tapisserie, Wandteppich.
my eyes were blurred: ich sah alles verschwommen.
13 **to depict:** darstellen.
14 **chariot:** (Streit-)Wagen.
14 f. **warrior:** Krieger.
15 **spiky:** stechend.
20 **obscured:** verdunkelt, dunkel, undeutlich.
21 f. **to cringe at s.o.'s feet:** vor jdm. am Boden kriechen.

reus' feet and she was pleading for mercy. Philomela. In the next scene he had advanced on her. He cut out her tongue. In the following scene Philomela, imprisoned in a castle, looked out as Tereus galloped away into the distance. That was all. I looked again. There was no doubt about it. Philomela.

I went to my room and sat holding the tapestry. Tereus' feet sounded in the courtyard outside: I pushed the tapestry under the couch and sat there as I had for so long, doing nothing. But he didn't come in.

So I was able to form my plan. I sent for Coda and Dita. I told them my suspicions and I gave the last of my gold for the search. Somewhere, between here and Athens, Philomela suffered alone. Secretly, men were found and set out on their horses. It was late at night when they left, and my heart beat loudly as I listened to the hooves growing fainter on the plain.

They found her and brought her back. Poor, dumb Philomela. And we all feasted, the smoke from the burning flesh of the animals went up into the sky for hours before we ate, the fountain was fed with wine, Tereus kept laughing and saying he must have made a mistake. He was so frightened he couldn't even find an excuse. So we ate and drank, and the wild boars on our gold cups chased themselves endlessly round as the gold glinted in the light from the torches and the round

2 **to advance on s.o.:** auf jdn. losgehen.
17 **hoof** (pl. *hooves*): Huf.
19 **to feast:** ein Fest begehen; ein Festmahl halten.
24 **boar:** Eber.
25 **to chase:** jagen.
26 **to glint:** glänzen, glitzern.

heads of Tereus' friends shone the same bright colour. Philomela never once looked reproach.
We lay together in my room, and I whispered in her ear. Her eyes could always answer me. And we knew we would avenge ourselves on Tereus.

Philomela lay in the prow of the boat. Her black hair just touched the water. I watched her all the time – for signs of happiness, or discontent, or simply to see what her eyes would say to me. Today she was smiling, and we glided at the rhythm of her breathing over water so clear that the smallest pebbles on the bottom looked as big and white as rocks.
We were there because a war was raging inland. On the shore, brightly coloured as victory, were Tereus' tents. From the beach little wisps of black smoke went up: the slaves were preparing the evening meal.
Tereus comes back from the war tonight. His fingers will pull at roasted meat. His mouth will be red with juice. The singing will start in a dull roar, and torches will be lit on the sand. Dancing figures, giants inside the tents but small in the great expanse outside, will run from every angle to the edge of the sea. Because of the wine, the moon will shine brilliantly.
The four curved paddles of our boat guided us gently

2 **to look reproach:** vorwurfsvoll dreinschauen.
5 **to avenge o.s. on s.o.:** sich an jdm. rächen.
6 **prow:** Bug.
11 **pebble:** Kieselstein.
15 **wisp:** (Rauch-)Wölkchen.
20 **giant:** Riese.
24 **curved:** geschwungen.

back to land. I stepped out, with Philomela in my arms, and set her down on the stones. We both stood for a moment, looking at the tents and the blade of blue which carves out the clumsy shapes of the mountains; but we saw only the evening ahead. It was months since Tereus had gone to the war. We had almost forgotten his face. He had gone, probably, because the embarrassment was too great for him at home – and he hoped, while he was away, that we would forget what he had done. We thought of him as we walked up to the encampment. And without glancing at each other again, we went to lie down until the heat of the day had passed.

The sun lay to one side of the sky and our shadows were long when we left the great tent and went inland to the olive groves. The preparations for the banquet were growing more frantic – and it was only when we were surrounded by bushes of myrtle and thyme that we were able to go on without vomiting on the ground. The smell of burning meat was so strong.

Philomela saw Itylus first. I followed the line of her pointing finger and could just make out, in the gloom where the trees were thicker, a group of boys playing at war. Itylus had a bow and arrow, and was running im-

4 **to carve out:** herausmeißeln.
11 **encampment:** Feldlager.
16 **grove:** Hain.
banquet: Bankett, Festmahl.
17 **frantic:** hektisch.
18 **myrtle:** Myrte.
thyme: Thymian.
22 **gloom:** Dunkel.

portantly from tree to tree calling out commands. As Tereus' son he was obeyed: this had made him arrogant, but charming still; already he had taken on the pompous, exaggerated stride of his father.

Now he sent a shower of arrows over our heads and the other boys ran laughing towards us to retrieve them. They all liked Philomela, and made a pretence of searching in the glade at her feet so she could stroke them and smile. And she did! While my heart beat heavily and slowly, and my legs felt as rooted and shapeless as the lines of trees that marched out to all sides of us.

Itylus!

I had to call him, of course – but if only it could have been Philomela! What do you want?

Anything to have been spared the sound of his voice. As I made no sign of moving, he came reluctantly forward. He knew I had come to spoil his game. It's nearly dark, I said. Your father is coming. We must go back to the tents.

He shrugged, then followed. We went in single file down to the beach.

Tereus will come down the mountain pass as the sun is setting. Taking advantage of the glory; wearing the flaming sky like a cloak he has picked up on the bat-

4 **pompous:** großspurig.
stride: Schreiten, Gangart.
6 **to retrieve:** zurückholen.
8 **glade:** Schneise, freie Stelle.
21 **to shrug:** die Achseln zucken.
in single file: im Gänsemarsch, eine(r) hinter dem, der Anderen.
25 **cloak:** Umhang, Mantel.

tlefield. Boasting as he tramps through the encampment. Flinging himself down, the exhausted warrior, and waiting for us, my tongueless sister and his wife to shower our praise on him.

On the pretext of showing him a big sea animal that had been caught in the nets that morning, we took Itylus into the cave at the other end of the beach. It was dark there, with a rancid smell: the colour of the air was the same deep grey all the way up to the roof of the cave and the rocks were thin and sharp like the teeth of a rotting fish. The children made piles of the fragile sea anemones and we crunched them under foot as we walked, the shells the faint pink-blue of an earlobe. Philomela and I stood silently by as Itylus, with controlled excitement, examined the monster.

A great eye lay in a network of tentacles. The confused limbs, sprawled now on the stale sand at the back of the cave, had evidently put up a fight – here and there they had been hacked by mens' hands and were crushed like a reed that someone has tried to break off and then abandoned. Perhaps because of the eye, which seemed, wherever we stood, to be watching us, we were afraid

2 **to fling o.s. down:** sich zu Boden werfen.
5 **pretext:** Vorwand.
8 **rancid:** ranzig.
11 **fragile:** zart, zerbrechlich.
12 **to crunch:** mit einem knirschenden Geräusch zertreten.
13 **earlobe:** Ohrläppchen.
16 **tentacle:** Tentakel, Fangarm.
17 (*to be*) **sprawled:** ausgebreitet liegen.
stale: alt, muffig.
20 **reed:** Schilfrohr.

to go too near. Only Itylus, to show his courage and manhood, picked up a piece of driftwood and advanced on it cautiously. It was dead since morning; but the glare of the black pupil in the pool of white suggested hidden power and energy. In our minds, we saw it rise and attack. The limbs, although twisted and battered, had a febrile strength. We felt them crush our ribs and wind themselves round our necks.

We lifted a boulder and came up on Itylus from behind. He fell without a sound. Philomela's eyes spoke terror. I was the only one to cry out.

The sound I made was flung back by the walls of the cave in anger and contempt. It took a long time to die, lingering in a whimper in the wet stone.

The eye still watched us as we lifted the body of Itylus and crept to the mouth of the cave with it. I looked out first. The sun was setting, the sky was red. I could see nothing of the black mountains, but a contingent of men, torches lit in preparation for the sudden descent of night, were moving like fiery beetles from the beach to the foothills. Tereus must be on his way down, then.

How quick and how slow our dragging of the great pot

2 **driftwood:** Treibholz.
4 **glare:** Schein, Glanz.
6 **to batter:** zerschmettern, -schlagen.
7 **febrile:** fiebrig.
9 **boulder:** Felsbrocken.
12 **to fling s.th. back:** etwas zurückwerfen, reflektieren.
13 **to die:** verhallen, -ebben.
14 **whimper:** Wimmern.
18 **contingent:** Anzahl.
19 **descent:** Hereinbrechen, Einbruch.

from its hiding place in the entrance of the cave, our pyre of dry wood, the heating of the water. But when we looked out at the sea, we saw his floating hair. And the sand in the red glow from the sinking sun was the colour of his poor boiling flesh. How slow!

Years and years will pass, and these minutes will still be longer than them all. Every hour will be made up out of them. And we will be standing by the staring eye in the back of the cave and Tereus will be coming down the hill and we will be standing at the mouth of the cave and looking out at the sea to shift the time. How quickly the years will pass!

When the meat was ready we drained the water away until there was only a little at the bottom of the pot. We had tried to find fresh water – there was an old well just above the beach – but seawater had seeped in. Tiny limpets and shreds of sour weed clung to the flesh. We threw in herbs and animal fat. Philomela made a dough with her agile fingers, which she used for speaking now, holding them up and flashing combinations of numbers when she had to make it clear what she wanted. I watched her hands as she laid the fine crust over the pot. We built up the fire, and waited.

2 **pyre:** Scheiterhaufen.
11 **to shift the time:** (sich) die Zeit vertreiben.
13 **to drain:** (Wasser) abgießen.
16 **to seep in:** einsickern.
17 **limpet:** Napfschnecke.
shred: Fetzen, Stück.
weed: *seaweed:* Tang.
18 **dough:** Teig.
19 **agile:** wendig, beweglich, geschickt.

It was a fine banquet. I sat at Tereus' side, my eyes down, my face flushed with pride for him. Philomela, as always on these occasions, was a ghost, a shadow that fell only occasionally across his face if he should look round and see her. I was his wife; and I celebrated his victories with him.

The men shouted and sang. When the moon rose, some of them ran drunkenly to the entrance to the tent, and gazed up at it as if it had appeared for the first time. Like Tereus, I laughed indulgently at them. Like Tereus, I applauded when the captive slave girls danced, their bodies greased and jewels shining between their eyes. With Tereus I rose and walked to the great table where the wine and food was laid out. On the glistening fig leaves, grapes and pomegranates stood in mounds. Great sides of roasted ox were garlanded with fast-wilting flowers.

The pie was brought in. Tereus sat down like a child and ate. When he had eaten a few mouthfuls, he nodded his approval. He offered some to his favourites, and they swaggered forward, holding out their hands. Then he turned to me.

10 **indulgently** (adv.): nachsichtig.
11 **captive:** gefangen (genommen).
12 **greased:** eingeölt, -gefettet.
14 **to glisten:** glänzen.
15 **fig:** Feige.
pomegrenate: Granatapfel.
mound: Hügel.
16 **to garland s.th.:** etwas bekränzen, schmücken.
16 f. **fast-wilting:** schnell welkend.
21 **to swagger:** stolzieren; taumeln.

Eat! – he said. You have done well.

I shook my head. Black, dizzy sickness. Inside me an ill-tempered sea rolled violently. I had to look up. Eyes looked back at me with a mixture of curiosity and dislike. Where is Philomela?

But her eyes had gone. And I half fell, as all the eyes there in that room merged together and one eye, lidless, staring shone out at me. Tereus, the juice from the pie dribbing down his chin, pulled me back on the seat beside him with astonishment. He thrust a tender morsel in my face. Eat! he said laughing. What's the matter with you?

Philomela came forward from the back of the tent. Because she was dumb the men were afraid of her, and they fell back easily enough to let her through. I felt Tereus wince.

Take that woman away! he muttered. But his voice lacked conviction: like the others, he was afraid of her. She had become, in the camp, like the priestess of an oracle without a voice. She was the unconscious avenger of every sin. If only Tereus knew the barbarity she had suffered, the others guessed at it.

2 **dizzy:** schwindlig.
3 **ill-tempered:** zornig.
7 **to merge together:** ineinander verschwimmen, miteinander verschmelzen.
9 **to drib:** tropfen.
10 **to thrust:** schieben.
10 f. **morsel:** Stückchen.
16 **to wince:** zusammenzucken.
17 **to mutter:** murmeln.
21 **avenger:** Rächer(in).
barbarity: Unmenschlichkeit, Grausamkeit.

She reached my side and took my hand so I could rise with new strength. Except for distant shouting outside, her silence had spread. The eyes looked at us now with fear and unease. They were waiting: waiting for me to speak.

I turned to Tereus.

It is for you to eat your son Itylus, I said. You destroyed us long ago.

(How slow! Tereus' long years of exile and grief. How quickly the years will pass.)

4 **unease:** Zweifel, Unbehagen.

Angela Carter

The Company of Wolves

One beast and only one howls in the woods by night.

The wolf is carnivore incarnate and he's as cunning as he is ferocious; once he's had a taste of flesh then nothing else will do.

At night, the eyes of wolves shine like candle flames, yellowish, reddish, but that is because the pupils of their eyes fatten on darkness and catch the light from your lantern to flash it back to you – red for danger; if a wolf's eyes reflect only moonlight, then they gleam a cold and unnatural green, a mineral, a piercing colour. If the benighted traveller spies those luminous, terrible sequins stitched suddenly on the black thickets, then he knows he must run, if fear has not struck him stock-still.

4 **The wolf is carnivore incarnate:** Der Wolf ist von Natur aus ein Fleischfresser, Raubtier.
cunning: schlau.
5 **ferocious:** wild.
9 **to fatten on s.th.:** sich bei etwas weiten.
11 **to gleam:** aufleuchten, erstrahlen lassen.
12 **piercing:** durchdringend.
13 **benighted:** unwissend.
luminous: leuchtend.
14 **sequin:** Paillette; auch: Zechine (alte venezianische Goldmünze).
to stitch: heften, sticken.
thicket: Dickicht.

But those eyes are all you will be able to glimpse of the forest assassins as they cluster invisibly round your smell of meat as you go through the wood unwisely late. They will be like shadows, they will be like wraiths, grey members of a congregation of nightmare; hark! his long, wavering howl ... an aria of fear made audible.

The wolfsong is the sound of the rending you will suffer, in itself a murdering.

It is winter and cold weather. In this region of mountain and forest, there is now nothing for the wolves to eat. Goats and sheep are locked up in the byre, the deer departed for the remaining pasturage on the southern slopes – wolves grow lean and famished. There is so little flesh on them that you could count the starveling ribs through their pelts, if they gave you time before they pounced. Those slavering jaws; the lolling

2 **assassin:** Mörder, Killer.
to cluster: sich versammeln, drängen.
5 **wraith:** Geist, Gespenst.
6 **hark!:** horch(t)!
to waver: zittern (Ton).
aria: Arie, Gesang.
7 **audible:** hörbar.
8 **rending:** Zerreißen, Zerrissenwerden.
12 **byre:** (Kuh-)Stall.
13 **pasturage:** Weide(land), -fläche.
14 **famished:** halb verhungert, ausgehungert.
15 f. **starveling:** abgezehrt, verkümmert, kläglich.
16 **pelt:** Fell.
17 **to pounce:** sich (auf sein Opfer) stürzen, zuschlagen.
to slaver: geifern.
to loll: heraushängen.

tongue; the rime of saliva on the grizzled chops – of all the teeming perils of the night and the forest, ghosts, hobgoblins, ogres that grill babies upon gridirons, witches that fatten their captives in cages for cannibal tables, the wolf is worst for he cannot listen to reason.

You are always in danger in the forest, where no people are. Step between the portals of the great pines where the shaggy branches tangle about you, trapping the unwary traveller in nets as if the vegetation itself were in a plot with the wolves who live there, as though the wicked trees go fishing on behalf of their friends – step between the gateposts of the forest with the greatest trepidation and infinite precautions, for if you stray from the path for one instant, the wolves will eat you. They are grey as famine, they are as unkind as plague.

1 **rime:** Rauhreif.
saliva: Speichel.
grizzled: grauhaarig.
chop: Kiefer, Maul.
2 **to teem:** wimmeln.
peril: Gefahr.
3 **hobgoblin:** Kobold.
ogre: Ungeheuer, Unhold.
gridiron: Gitter-, Bratrost.
4 **witch:** Hexe.
captive: Gefangene(r).
9 **shaggy:** zottelig, struppig.
to tangle: umschlingen.
9 f. **unwary:** unvorsichtig, unbedacht.
14 **trepidation:** Angst, Beklommenheit.
14 f. **to stray from the path:** vom Weg abkommen, sich verirren.
16 **famine:** Hungersnot.
plague: Pest.

The grave-eyed children of the sparse villages always carry knives with them when they go out to tend the little flocks of goats that provide the homesteads with acrid milk and rank, maggoty cheeses. Their knives are half as big as they are, the blades are sharpened daily.

But the wolves have ways of arriving at your own hearthside. We try and try but sometimes we cannot keep them out. There is no winter's night the cottager does not fear to see a lean, grey, famished snout questing under the door, and there was a woman once bitten in her own kitchen as she was straining the macaroni.

Fear and flee the wolf; for, worst of all, the wolf may be more than he seems.

There was a hunter once, near here, that trapped a wolf in a pit. This wolf had massacred the sheep and goats; eaten up a mad old man who used to live by himself in a hut halfway up the mountain and sing to Jesus all day; pounced on a girl looking after the sheep, but she made such a commotion that men came with rifles and scared

1 **sparse:** dünn (gesät) (Besiedlung).
3 **flock:** Herde.
homestead: Haus, Heim.
4 **acrid:** sauer.
rank: stinkend.
maggotty: voller Maden.
8 **hearthside:** Herd, Feuerstelle.
9 **cottager:** Häusler.
10 **snout:** Schnauze.
10 f. **to quest:** suchen, stöbern.
12 **to strain:** sieben, abgießen.
21 **commotion:** Aufruhr.

him away and tried to track him into the forest but he was cunning and easily gave them the slip. So this hunter dug a pit and put a duck in it, for bait, all alive-oh; and he covered the pit with straw smeared with wolf dung. Quack, quack! went the duck and a wolf came slinking out of the forest, a big one, a heavy one, he weighed as much as a grown man and the straw gave way beneath him – into the pit he tumbled. The hunter jumped down after him, slit his throat, cut off all his paws for a trophy.

And then no wolf at all lay in front of the hunter but the bloody trunk of a man, headless, footless, dying, dead.

A witch from up the valley once turned an entire wedding party into wolves because the groom had settled on another girl. She used to order them to visit her, at night, from spite, and they would sit and howl around her cottage for her, serenading her with their misery.

Not so very long ago, a young woman in our village married a man who vanished clean away on her wedding night. The bed was made with new sheets and the bride lay down in it; the groom said, he was going out to relieve himself, insisted on it, for the sake of de-

2 **to give s.o. the slip:** jdm. entwischen.
3 **bait:** Köder.
6 **to slink:** schleichen.
8 **to tumble:** fallen, plumpsen.
9 **to slit:** aufschlitzen.
10 **paw:** Pfote.
15 **groom:** *bridegroom:* Bräutigam.
18 **to serenade s.o.:** jdm. ein Ständchen bringen.
23 f. **decency:** Anstand, Schicklichkeit.

cency, and she drew the coverlet up to her chin and she lay there. And she waited and she waited and then she waited again – surely he's been gone a long time? Until she jumps up in bed and shrieks to hear a howling, coming on the wind from the forest.

That long-drawn, wavering howl has, for all its fearful resonance, some inherent sadness in it, as if the beasts would love to be less beastly if only they knew how and never cease to mourn their own condition. There is a vast melancholy in the canticles of the wolves, melancholy infinite as the forest, endless as these long nights of winter and yet that ghastly sadness, that mourning for their own, irremediable appetites, can never move the heart for not one phrase in it hints at the possibility of redemption; grace could not come to the wolf from its own despair, only through some external mediator, so that, sometimes, the beast will look as if he half welcomes the knife that despatches him.

The young woman's brothers searched the outhouses and the haystacks but never found any remains so the sensible girl dried her eyes and found herself another

1 **coverlet:** Bett-, Zudecke.
4 **to shriek:** aufschreien, kreischen.
7 **resonance:** Widerhall.
9 **to mourn:** betrauern.
10 **canticle:** (Lob-)Gesang.
12 **ghastly:** grässlich, gespenstisch.
13 **irremediable:** unabänderlich, unheilbar.
15 **redemption:** Erlösung.
16 **mediator:** Vermittler(in).
18 **to despatch:** töten, erledigen.
19 **outhouse:** Anbau, Nebengebäude.
20 **haystack:** Heuschober.

husband not too shy to piss into a pot who spent the nights indoors. She gave him a pair of bonny babies and all went right as a trivet until, one freezing night, the night of the solstice, the hinge of the year when things do not fit together as well as they should, the longest night, her first good man came home again.

A great thump on the door announced him as she was stirring the soup for the father of her children and she knew him the moment she lifted the latch to him although it was years since she'd worn black for him and now he was in rags and his hair hung down his back and never saw a comb, alive with lice.

"Here I am again, missus," he said. "Get me my bowl of cabbage and be quick about it."

Then her second husband came in with wood for the fire and when the first one saw she'd slept with another man and, worse, clapped his red eyes on her little children who'd crept into the kitchen to see what all the din was about, he shouted: "I wish I were a wolf again, to teach this whore a lesson!" So a wolf he instantly became and tore off the eldest boy's left foot before he was chopped up with the hatchet they used for chop-

2 **bonny:** herzig, süß.
3 **to go right as a trivet:** in schönster Ordnung sein.
freezing: frostig, eisig.
4 **solstice:** Sonnenwende.
hinge: (Tür-)Angel.
7 **thump:** (wuchtiger) Schlag; (heftiges) Pochen.
9 **latch:** Türriegel.
12 **louse** (pl. *lice*): Laus.
19 **din:** Lärm.
20 **whore:** Hure.
22 **hatchet:** Beil.

ping logs. But when the wolf lay bleeding and gasping its last, the pelt peeled off again and he was just as he had been, years ago, when he ran away from his marriage bed, so that she wept and her second husband beat her.

They say there's an ointment the Devil gives you that turns you into a wolf the minute you rub it on. Or, that he was born feet first and had a wolf for his father and his torso is a man's but his legs and genitals are a wolf's. And he has a wolf's heart.

Seven years is a werewolf's natural span but if you burn his human clothing you condemn him to wolfishness for the rest of his life, so old wives hereabouts think it some protection to throw a hat or an apron at the werewolf, as if clothes made the man. Yet by the eyes, those phosphorescent eyes, you know him in all his shapes; the eyes alone unchanged by metamorphosis.

Before he can become a wolf, the lycanthrope strips stark naked. If you spy a naked man among the pines, you must run as if the Devil were after you.

1 f. **to gasp one's last:** den letzten Atemzug tun.
6 **ointment:** Salbe.
9 **torso:** Torso, Rumpf, Oberkörper.
11 **werewolf:** Werwolf (im alten Volksglauben Mensch, der sich von Zeit zu Zeit in einen Wolf verwandelt und andere Menschen bedroht).
span: Lebenszeit, -erwartung.
14 **apron:** Schürze.
17 **metamorphosis:** Metamorphose, Verwandlung.
18 **lycanthrope:** Lykanthrop, Werwolf, Wolfsmensch.
19 **stark naked:** splitternackt.

It is midwinter and the robin, the friend of man, sits on the handle of the gardener's spade and sings. It is the worst time in all the year for wolves but this strong-minded child insists she will go off through the wood. She is quite sure the wild beasts cannot harm her although, well-warned, she lays a carving knife in the basket her mother has packed with cheeses. There is a bottle of harsh liquor distilled from brambles; a batch of flat oatcakes baked on the hearthstone; a pot or two of jam. The flaxen-haired girl will take these delicious gifts to a reclusive grandmother so old the burden of her years is crushing her to death. Granny lives two hours' trudge through the winter woods; the child wraps herself up in her thick shawl, draws it over her head. She steps into her stout wooden shoes; she is dressed and ready and it is Christmas Eve. The malign door of the solstice still swings upon its hinges but she has been too much loved ever to feel scared.

1 **robin:** Rotkehlchen.
6 **carving knife:** Fleisch-, Tranchiermesser (*to carve:* [Fleisch] aufschneiden).
8 **harsh:** stark, scharf.
liquor: Schnaps.
to distil: destillieren, brennen.
bramble: Brombeere.
batch: Schub.
9 **oatcake:** (flacher) Haferkuchen.
10 **flaxen-haired:** flachs-, hellblond.
11 **reclusive:** abgeschieden lebend.
13 **trudge:** (Fuß-)Marsch.
14 **shawl:** Umschlagtuch.
15 **stout:** fest, robust.
16 **malign:** böse, unheilvoll.

Children do not stay young for long in this savage country. There are no toys for them to play with so they work hard and grow wise but this one, so pretty and the youngest of her family, a little late-comer, had been indulged by her mother and the grandmother who'd knitted her the red shawl that, today, has the ominous if brilliant look of blood on snow. Her breasts have just begun to swell; her hair is like lint, so fair it hardly makes a shadow on her pale forehead; her cheeks are an emblematic scarlet and white and she has just started her woman's bleeding, the clock inside her that will strike, henceforward, once a month.

She stands and moves within the invisible pentacle of her own virginity. She is an unbroken egg; she is a sealed vessel; she has inside her a magic space the entrance to which is shut tight with a plug of membrane; she is a closed system; she does not know how to shiver. She has her knife and she is afraid of nothing.

Her father might forbid her, if he were home, but he is away in the forest, gathering wood, and her mother cannot deny her.

The forest closed upon her like a pair of jaws.

There is always something to look at in the forest, even

6 **ominous:** unheilvoll, drohend.
8 **lint:** Linnen.
10 **emblematic:** symbolisch, zeichenhaft.
scarlet: Scharlachrot.
12 **henceforward:** von jetzt ab, an.
13 **pentacle:** Pentagramm, Drudenfuß (Zauberzeichen).
14 **virginity:** Jungfräulichkeit.
15 **vessel:** Gefäß.
17 **to shiver:** zittern, beben.

in the middle of winter – the huddled mounds of birds, succumbed to the lethargy of the season, heaped on the creaking boughs and too forlorn to sing; the bright frills of the winter fungi on the blotched trunks of the trees; the cuneiform slots of rabbits and deer, the herringbone tracks of the birds, a hare as lean as a rasher of bacon streaking across the path where the thin sunlight dapples the russet brakes of last year's bracken.

When she heard the freezing howl of a distant wolf, her practised hand sprang to the handle of her knife, but she saw no sign of a wolf at all, nor of a naked man, neither, but then she heard a clattering among the

1 **huddled:** hingekauert, zusammengedrängt.
mound: Hügel, Haufen.
2 **to succumb to s.th.:** einer Sache erliegen, von etwas besiegt sein.
lethargy: Lethargie, Trägheit.
3 **to creak:** knarren.
bough: Zweig, Ast.
forlorn: verzweifelt; einsam und verlassen.
4 **frill:** Krause, Rüsche.
fungus (pl. *fungi*): Pilz.
blotched: fleckig.
5 **cuneiform:** keilförmig.
slot: Schlitz, schlitzförmige Vertiefung.
6 **herringbone:** Fischgrät(muster).
hare: Hase.
7 **rasher:** (Speck-)Scheibe.
to streak: flitzen.
8 **to dapple:** (be)sprenkeln.
russet: rostbraun, -rot.
brake: Dickicht, Gestrüpp.
9 **bracken:** Farnkraut.
10 **to freeze** (fig.): erstarren lassen.
13 **clattering:** Lärm.

brushwood and there sprang on to the path a fully clothed one, a very handsome young one, in the green coat and wideawake hat of a hunter, laden with carcasses of game birds. She had her hand on her knife at the first rustle of twigs but he laughed with a flash of white teeth when he saw her and made her a comic yet flattering little bow; she'd never seen such a fine fellow before, not among the rustic clowns of her native village. So on they went together, through the thickening light of the afternoon.

Soon they were laughing and joking like old friends. When he offered to carry her basket, she gave it to him although her knife was in it because he told her his rifle would protect them. As the day darkened, it began to snow again; she felt the first flakes settle on her eyelashes but now there was only half a mile to go and there would be a fire, and hot tea, and a welcome, a warm one, surely, for the dashing huntsman as well as for herself.

This young man had a remarkable object in his pocket. It was a compass. She looked at the little round glass face in the palm of his hand and watched the wavering

1 **brushwood:** Unterholz.
3 **wideawake:** hier: weit ausladend.
3 f. **carcass:** Kadaver.
4 **game bird:** Federwild.
5 **rustle:** Rascheln.
7 **flattering:** schmeichelhaft; schmeichlerisch.
8 **rustic:** ländlich, tölpelhaft.
15 **flake:** (Schnee-)Flocke.
15 f. **eyelashes:** Wimpern.
18 **dashing:** schneidig.

needle with a vague wonder. He assured her this compass had taken him safely through the wood on his hunting trip because the needle always told him with perfect accuracy where the north was. She did not believe it; she knew she should never leave the path on the way through the wood or else she would be lost instantly. He laughed at her again; gleaming trails of spittle clung to his teeth. He said, if he plunged off the path into the forest that surrounded them, he could guarantee to arrive at her grandmother's house a good quarter of an hour before she did, plotting his way through the undergrowth with his compass, while she trudged the long way, along the winding path.

I don't believe you. Besides, aren't you afraid of the wolves?

He only tapped the gleaming butt of his rifle and grinned.

Is it a bet? he asked her. Shall we make a game of it? What will you give me if I get to your grandmother's house before you?

What would you like? she asked disingenuously.

A kiss.

Commonplaces of a rustic seduction; she lowered her eyes and blushed.

He went through the undergrowth and took her basket

7 f. **trails of spittle:** Speichelspuren, -tröpfchen.
8 **to plunge:** springen, stürzen, tauchen.
12 **to trudge:** stapfen.
16 **butt:** (Gewehr-)Kolben.
21 **disingenuously** (adv.): hinterhältig.
23 **commonplace:** Gemeinplatz, Floskel.
seduction: Verführung.

with him but she forgot to be afraid of the beasts, although now the moon was rising, for she wanted to dawdle on her way to make sure the handsome gentleman would win his wager.

Grandmother's house stood by itself a little way out of the village. The freshly falling snow blew in eddies about the kitchen garden and the young man stepped delicately up the snowy path to the door as if he were reluctant to get his feet wet, swinging his bundle of game and the girl's basket and humming a little tune to himself.

There is a faint trace of blood on his chin; he has been snacking on his catch.

He rapped upon the panels with his knuckles.

Aged and frail, granny is three-quarters succumbed to the mortality the ache in her bones promises her and almost ready to give in entirely. A boy came out from the village to build up her hearth for the night an hour ago and the kitchen crackles with busy firelight. She has her Bible for company, she is a pious old woman.

3 **to dawdle:** trödeln.
4 **wager:** Wette.
6 **eddy:** Wirbel.
10 **to hum:** summen.
13 **catch:** Fang, erlegtes Wild, Beute.
14 **to rap:** klopfen.
panels (pl.): Türfüllung.
15 **frail:** zerbrechlich, schwach.
16 **mortality:** Sterblichkeit.
18 **to build up the hearth:** den Herd, Ofen anschüren, -heizen.
19 **to crackle:** knistern, prasseln.
20 **pious:** fromm.

She is propped up on several pillows in the bed set into the wall peasant-fashion, wrapped up in the patchwork quilt she made before she was married, more years ago than she cares to remember. Two china spaniels with liver-coloured blotches on their coats and black noses sit on either side of the fireplace. There is a bright rug of woven rags on the pantiles. The grandfather clock ticks away her eroding time.

We keep the wolves outside by living well.

He rapped upon the panels with his hairy knuckles.

It is your granddaughter, he mimicked in a high soprano.

Lift up the latch and walk in, my darling.

You can tell them by their eyes, eyes of a beast of prey, nocturnal, devastating eyes as red as a wound; you can hurl your Bible at him and your apron after, granny, you thought that was a sure prophylactic against these infernal vermin ... now call on Christ and his mother and all the angels in heaven to protect you but it won't do you any good.

1 **to be propped up:** (mit dem Rücken an etwas gelehnt) sitzen.
3 **quilt:** Bettdecke.
5 **blotch:** Fleck.
7 **pantile:** eigtl.: Dachziegel, -pfanne; hier: Bodenziegel.
grandfather clock: Standuhr.
8 **to erode:** aushöhlen, aufzehren.
14 **beast of prey:** Raubtier.
15 **nocturnal:** nächtlich.
devastating: verheerend, vernichtend, überwältigend.
16 **to hurl:** schleudern.
17 **prophylactic:** Vorbeugungsmaßnahme, Abwehrmittel.
18 **infernal:** infernalisch, höllisch, teuflisch.
vermin: Schädlinge, Parasiten; Pack, Gesindel, Abschaum.

His feral muzzle is sharp as a knife; he drops his golden burden of gnawed pheasant on the table and puts down your dear girl's basket, too. Oh, my God, what have you done with her?

Off with his disguise, that coat of forest-coloured cloth, the hat with the feather tucked into the ribbon; his matted hair streams down his white shirt and she can see the lice moving in it. The sticks in the hearth shift and hiss; night and the forest has come into the kitchen with darkness tangled in its hair.

He strips off his shirt. His skin is the colour and texture of vellum. A crisp stripe of hair runs down his belly, his nipples are ripe and dark as poison fruit but he's so thin you could count the ribs under his skin if only he gave you the time. He strips off his trousers and she can see how hairy his legs are. His genitals, huge. Ah! huge.

The last thing the old lady saw in all this world was a young man, eyes like cinders, naked as a stone, approaching her bed.

The wolf is carnivore incarnate.

1 **feral:** wölfisch, wild.
muzzle: Schnauze.
2 **to gnaw:** (ab)nagen.
pheasant: Fasan.
6 **to tuck:** stecken.
6 f. **matted:** verfilzt.
9 **to hiss:** zischen.
10 **tangled:** verstrickt.
11 **texture:** Oberfläche, Struktur.
12 **vellum:** Pergament.
crisp: scharf (Umriß).
13 **nipple:** Brustwarze.
18 **cinder:** glühendes Stück Kohle.

When he had finished with her, he licked his chops and quickly dressed himself again, until he was just as he had been when he came through her door. He burned the inedible hair in the fireplace and wrapped the bones up in a napkin that he hid away under the bed in the wooden chest in which he found a clean pair of sheets. These he carefully put on the bed instead of the tell-tale stained ones he stowed away in the laundry basket. He plumped up the pillows and shook out the patchwork quilt, he picked up the Bible from the floor, closed it and laid it on the table. All was as it had been before except that grandmother was gone. The sticks twitched in the grate, the clock ticked and the young man sat patiently, deceitfully beside the bed in granny's nightcap.

Rat-a-tap-tap.

Who's there, he quavers in granny's antique falsetto.

Only your granddaughter.

So she came in, bringing with her a flurry of snow that melted in tears on the tiles, and perhaps she was a little disappointed to see only her grandmother sitting beside

4 **inedible:** ungenießbar, nicht essbar.
5 **napkin:** Serviette.
8 **tell-tale:** verräterisch.
9 **to plump up:** aufschütteln.
13 **to twitch:** zucken.
grate: Rost, Kamin.
14 **deceitfully** (adv.): falsch, hinterlistig.
17 **to quaver:** mit zitternder, zittriger Stimme sprechen.
falsetto: Fistelstimme.
19 **flurry:** (Schnee-)Gestöber.
20 **tiles:** Bodenfliesen.

the fire. But then he flung off the blanket and sprang to the door, pressing his back against it so that she could not get out again.

The girl looked round the room and saw there was not even the indentation of a head on the smooth cheek of the pillow and how, for the first time she'd seen it so, the Bible lay closed on the table. The tick of the clock cracked like a whip. She wanted her knife from her basket but she did not dare reach for it because his eyes were fixed upon her – huge eyes that now seemed to shine with a unique, interior light, eyes the size of saucers, saucers full of Greek fire, diabolic phosphorescence.

What big eyes you have.

All the better to see you with.

No trace at all of the old woman except for a tuft of white hair that had caught in the bark of an unburned log. When the girl saw that, she knew she was in danger of death.

Where is my grandmother?

There's nobody here but we two, my darling.

Now a great howling rose up all around them, near, very near, as close as the kitchen garden, the howling of a multitude of wolves; she knew the worst wolves are hairy on the inside and she shivered, in spite of the

1 **to fling off:** zurückwerfen, -schleudern.
5 **indentation:** Einkerbung, Abdruck.
12 **Greek fire:** von den Byzantinern bei Seeschlachten und noch in den Kriegen des Mittelalters verwendeter Brandsatz.
12 f. **phosphorescence:** Phosphorschimmer, grünes Flackern.
16 **tuft:** Büschel.
24 **multitude:** Menge.

scarlet shawl she pulled more closely round herself as if it could protect her although it was as red as the blood she must spill.

Who has come to sing us carols, she said.

Those are the voices of my brothers, darling; I love the company of wolves. Look out of the window and you'll see them.

Snow half-caked the lattice and she opened it to look into the garden. It was a white night of moon and snow; the blizzard whirled round the gaunt, grey beasts who squatted on their haunches among the rows of winter cabbage, pointing their sharp snouts to the moon and howling as if their hearts would break. Ten wolves; twenty wolves – so many wolves she could not count them, howling in concert as if demented or deranged. Their eyes reflected the light from the kitchen and shone like a hundred candles.

It is very cold, poor things, she said; no wonder they howl so.

She closed the window on the wolves' threnody and

3 **to spill:** vergießen.
4 **carol:** (fröhliches) Lied.
8 **to half-cake:** halb verkrusten, verschließen.
lattice: Gitter.
10 **to whirl:** wirbeln.
gaunt: hager.
11 **to squat:** hocken.
haunch: Hinterpfote.
15 **demented:** wahnsinnig, verrückt.
deranged: geistesgestört.
20 **threnody:** rituelle Totenklage (im Griechenland der Antike), Klagelied.

took off her scarlet shawl, the colour of poppies, the colour of sacrifices, the colour of her menses, and, since her fear did her no good, she ceased to be afraid.

What shall I do with my shawl?

Throw it on the fire, dear one. You won't need it again.

She bundled up her shawl and threw it on the blaze, which instantly consumed it. Then she drew her blouse over her head; her small breasts gleamed as if the snow had invaded the room.

What shall I do with my blouse?

Into the fire with it, too, my pet.

The thin muslin went flaring up the chimney like a magic bird and now off came her skirt, her woollen stockings, her shoes, and on to the fire they went, too, and were gone for good. The firelight shone through the edges of her skin; now she was clothed only in her untouched integument of flesh. This dazzling, naked she combed out her hair with her fingers; her hair looked white as the snow outside. Then went directly to the man with red eyes in whose unkempt mane the lice moved; she stood up on tiptoe and unbuttoned the collar of his shirt.

1 **poppy:** Klatschmohn.
2 **menses** (pl.): Monatsblutung.
7 **blaze:** loderndes Feuer.
13 **muslin:** Musselin (dünner Baumwollstoff).
to flare up: aufflammen, -lodern.
18 **integument:** Hülle, Haut.
to dazzle: blenden.
21 **unkempt:** ungekämmt, ungepflegt.
mane: Mähne.
22 **on tiptoe:** auf Zehenspitzen.

What big arms you have.

All the better to hug you with.

Every wolf in the world now howled a prothalamion outside the window as she freely gave the kiss she owed him.

What big teeth you have!

She saw how his jaw began to slaver and the room was full of the clamour of the forest's Liebestod but the wise child never flinched, even when he answered:

All the better to eat you with.

The girl burst out laughing; she knew she was nobody's meat. She laughed at him full in the face, she ripped off his shirt for him and flung it into the fire, in the fiery wake of her own discarded clothing. The flames danced like dead souls on Walpurgisnacht and the old bones under the bed set up a terrible clattering but she did not pay them any heed.

Carnivore incarnate, only immaculate flesh appeases him.

She will lay his fearful head on her lap and she will pick out the lice from his pelt and perhaps she will put the

3 **prothalamion:** Hochzeitslied, -gesang.

8 **clamour:** Geschrei.

Liebestod: Anspielung auf »Isoldes Liebestod«, berühmte Arie in Richard Wagners Oper *Tristan und Isolde* (1865).

9 **to flinch:** zurückschrecken, -zucken.

12 **to rip off:** wegreißen.

14 **to discard:** (Kleidung) ablegen.

15 **Walpurgisnacht:** legendärer Hexensabbat, bei dem die Hexen sich auf dem Brocken im Harz zum Tanz versammeln.

17 **to pay heed to s.th.:** auf etwas achten.

18 **immaculate:** unbefleckt, makellos, rein.

to appease: besänftigen, beschwichtigen.

lice into her mouth and eat them, as he will bid her, as she would do in a savage marriage ceremony.

The blizzard will die down.

The blizzard died down, leaving the mountains as randomly covered with snow as if a blind woman had thrown a sheet over them, the upper branches of the forest pines limed, creaking, swollen with the fall.

Snowlight, moonlight, a confusion of paw-prints.

All silent, all still.

Midnight; and the clock strikes. It is Christmas Day, the werewolves' birthday, the door of the solstice stands wide open; let them all sink through.

See! sweet and sound she sleeps in granny's bed, between the paws of the tender wolf.

7 **limed: 1.** mit Vogelleim bestrichen; **2.** mit Kalk bestäubt.
fall: (Schnee-)Fall, Niederschlag(smenge).

Fay Weldon

In the Great War

Enid's mother Patty didn't stand a chance. That was in the Great War, in the fifties, when women were at war with women. Victory meant a soft bed and an easy life: defeat meant loneliness and the humiliation of the spinster. These days, of course, women have declared themselves allies, and united in a new war, a cold war, against the common enemy, man. But then, in the Great War, things were very different. And Patty didn't stand a chance against Helene. She was, for one thing, badly equipped for battle. Her legs were thick and practical, her breasts floppy, and her features, though pleasant enough, lacked erotic impact. Her blue eyes were watery and her hair frizzy and cut brusquely for easy washing and combing. "I can't stand all this dolling up," she'd say. "What's the point?"

2 **Great War:** Erster Weltkrieg.
3 **to stand a chance:** eine Chance haben.
6 **humiliation:** Demütigung, Herabsetzung.
7 **spinster:** alte Jungfer.
8 **ally:** Verbündete(r).
13 **floppy:** schlaff.
15 **frizzy:** kraus.
brusquely (adv.): rigoros.
16 f. **dolling up:** puppenhafte Aufmachung, Aufgetakeltsein.
17 **what's the point?** (coll.): wozu?, was soll das?

Patty cooked with margarine because it was cheaper than butter and her white sauces were always lumpy. She wouldn't keep pot plants, or souvenirs, or even a cat. What was the point?

She didn't like sex and, though she never refused her husband Arthur, she washed so carefully before and after, she made him feel he must have been really rather dirty.

Patty, in other words, was what she was, and saw no point in pretending to be anything else. Or in cooking with mushrooms or holidaying abroad or buying a new pair of shoes for Enid, her only child, when she had a perfectly good pair already, or going with her husband to the pub. And, indeed, there very often was no point in these things, except surely life must be more than something just to be practically and sensibly *got through*?

Enid thought so. Enid thought she'd do better than her mother in the Great War. Enid buffed her pre-pubertal nails and arranged wild flowers in jam jars and put them on the kitchen table. Perhaps she could see what was coming!

For all Patty's good qualities – cleanliness, honesty, thrift, reliability, kindness, sobriety, and so on – did her

2 **lumpy:** klumpig.
19 **to buff:** auf Hochglanz polieren, putzen.
pre-pubertal: vorpubertär.
23 **cleanliness:** Reinlichkeit.
24 **thrift:** Sparsamkeit.
reliability: Zuverlässigkeit.
sobriety: Nüchternheit.

no good whatsoever when Helene came along. Or so Enid observed. Patty was asleep on duty, and there all of a sudden was Helene, the enemy at the gate, with her slim legs and her bedroom eyes, enticing Arthur away. "But what does she *see* in Arthur?" asked Patty, dumbfounded. What you don't! the ten-year-old Enid thought, but did not say.

In fact, the Second World Male War, from 1939 to 1945, which men had waged among themselves in the name of Democracy, Freedom, Racial Supremacy and so forth, to the great detriment of women and children everywhere, had sharpened the savagery of the Female War. There just weren't enough men to go around. In ordinary times Helene would have gone into battle for some unmarried professional man – accountant or executive – but having lost country, home, family and friends in the ruins of Berlin now laid claim to Arthur, Patty's husband, a railway engineer in the north of England, who painted portraits as a hobby. The battle she fought for him was short and

4 **to entice:** locken.
6 **dumbfounded:** verblüfft, sprachlos.
9 **to wage:** (Krieg) führen.
10 **supremacy:** Überlegenheit, Vorherrschaft.
11 **detriment:** Schaden.
12 **savagery:** Vehemenz, Grausamkeit.
13 f. **enough men to go around:** genug Männer für alle (*to go around:* reichen, langen).
15 **professional man:** Mann mit qualifiziertem Beruf; höherer Angestellter; Akademiker.
16 **accountant:** (Bilanz-)Buchhalter; Wirtschaftsprüfer.
executive: leitender Angestellter, Geschäftsführer.

sharp. She shaved her shapely legs and flashed her liquid eyes.

"She's no better than a whore," said Patty. "Shaving her legs!" If God put hairs on your legs, thought Patty, then a woman's duty, and her husband's, too, is to put up with them.

Helene thought otherwise. And in her eyes Arthur saw the promise of secret bliss, the complicity of abandon, and all the charm of sin: the pink of her rosy nipples suffused the new world she offered him. And so, without much difficulty Helene persuaded Arthur to leave Patty and Enid, give up his job, paint pictures for a living and think the world well lost for love.

By some wonderful fluke – wonderful, that is, for Arthur and Helene, if infuriating for Patty – Arthur's paintings were an outstanding commercial success. They became the worst bestselling paintings of the sixties, and Arthur, safely divorced from Patty, lived happily ever after with Helene, painting the occasional painting of wide-eyed deer, and sipping champagne by

1 **shapely:** wohlgeformt.
2 **liquid:** glänzend (Augen).
3 **whore:** Hure.
8 **bliss:** Glück(seligkeit).
complicity: Komplizenschaft.
abandon: Hingabe.
9 **nipple:** Brustwarze.
10 **to suffuse:** überschwemmen.
13 **to think the world well lost:** etwa: der Welt Ade sagen.
14 **by a fluke:** durch einen glücklichen Zufall.
15 **to infuriate:** erzürnen, wütend machen.
20 **to sip s.th.:** etwas in kleinen Schlucken trinken, an etwas nippen.

the side of swimming pools. "Nasty acidy stuff, champagne," said Patty.

Enid – Patty and Arthur's daughter – never really forgave her mother for losing the war. As if poor Patty didn't have enough to put up with already, without being blamed by her daughter for something she could hardly help! But that's the way these things go – life is the opposite of fair. It stuns you one moment and trips your feet from under you the next, and then jumps up and down on you, pound, pound, pound for good measure.

You should have seen Enid, when she was twelve, twisting the knife in her mother's wounds, poking about among the lumps of the cauliflower cheese, saying: "Do we *have* to eat this? No wonder Dad left home!" "Eat it up, it's good for you," her mother would reply. "If you want something fancy go and live with your stepmother."

And, indeed, Enid had been asked, but Enid never went. Enid would twist a knife but not deliver a mortal wound, not to her mother. Instead she took up the

1 **acidy:** sauer, ätzend.
8 **to stun:** betäuben, verblüffen.
10 **pound:** etwa: wum! (*to pound:* hämmern, donnern, stampfen).
10 f. **for good measure:** zusätzlich.
13 f. **to poke about:** herumstochern.
14 **cauliflower cheese:** Blumenkohl mit Käsesauce.
17 **something fancy:** etwas Ausgefallenes.
18 **stepmother:** Stiefmutter.

armoury her mother never wore, breathed on it, burnished it, sharpened its cutting edges, prepared for war herself. Long after the war was over, Enid was still fighting. She was like some mad Aussie soldier hiding out in the Malayan jungle, still looking for a foe that had years since thrown away its grenades and taken to TV assembly instead.

At sixteen Enid scanned the fashion pages and read hints on make-up and how to be an interesting person; she went weekly to the theatre and art galleries and classical music concerts and exercised every day, and not until she was eighteen did she feel properly prepared to step into the battlefield. She was intelligent, and thought it sensible enough to go to university, although she chose English literature as the subject least likely to put men off.

"Nothing puts a man off like a clever woman," said Helene when Enid visited. Now warriors in the Great War thought nothing of swapping secrets. Intelligence ser-

1 **armoury:** Rüstung.
to breathe: hauchen.
1 f. **to burnish:** polieren.
4 **Aussie** (coll.): *Australian.*
5 **jungle:** Dschungel.
foe: Feind.
6 **grenade:** (Hand-)Granate.
7 **TV assembly:** TV-Montage.
11 **to exercise:** Sport, Gymnastik machen.
16 **to put s.o. off:** jdn. abschrecken.
19 **to swap:** austauschen, sich gegenseitig erzählen.

vices of warring countries, hand in glove, glove in hand! It's always been so. Just as there's always been trade with enemy nations, unofficially if not officially. Helene lisped out quite a few secrets to Enid: her accent tinged with all the poise and decadence of a vanished Europe. "My foreign wife!" Arthur would say, proudly in his honest, northern, jovial, middle-aged voice. Arthur was the J. B. Priestley of the art world – good in spite of himself.

Oh, Patty had lost a lovely prize, Enid knew it! Her beloved father! What a victory Patty's could have been – and yet she chose defeat. She'd chosen a bra to flatten an already flat chest. "What's the point?" she asked, when Enid said she was going off to university. Couldn't she even see that?

Little Enid, so bright and knowledgeable and determined! So young, so ruthless – a warrior! And fortune favours the brave, the strong, the ruthless. That was the point. Enid's professor, Walter Walther, looked at Enid

1 **hand in glove:** (fig.) unter einer Decke.
4 **to lisp out:** zuwispern.
4 f. (*to be*) **tinged with s.th.:** (fig.) eine leichte Färbung von etwas, einen Anklang an etwas haben, nicht ganz frei von etwas sein.
5 **poise:** Selbstsicherheit.
decadence: Dekadenz, Überfeinerung.
8 **Priestley:** John Boynton P. (1894-1984), englischer Schriftsteller.
12 **bra:** BH.
16 **knowledgeable:** beschlagen, kundig, wissend.
17 **ruthless:** unbarmherzig, mitleidlos.
warrior: Krieger(in), Kämpfer(in).

in a lingering way, and Enid looked straight back. Take me! Well, not quite take me. Love me now, take me eventually.

Walter Walther was forty-eight. Enid was nineteen. Enid was studying Chaucer. Enid said in an essay that Chaucer's Parfait Gentle Knight was no hero but a crude mercenary, and Chaucer, in his adulation, was being ironic; Walter Walther hadn't thought of that before, and at forty-eight it is delightful to meet someone who says something you haven't thought of before. And she was so young, and dewy, almost downy, so that if she was out in the rain the drops lay like silver balls upon her skin; and she was surprisingly knowledgeable for one so young, and knew all about music and painting, which Walter didn't, much, and she had an interesting, rich father, if a rather dowdy, vague, distant little mother. And Enid was warm.

Oh, Enid was warm! Enid was warm against his body on stolen nights. Walter's wife Rosanne, four years

1 **lingering:** sehnsuchtsvoll.
5 **Chaucer:** Geoffrey Ch. (um 1340-1400), mittelenglischer Dichter; begann um 1386 sein berühmtestes Werk *The Canterbury Tales*, das um 1478 gedruckt wurde.
6 **Parfait Gentle Knight:** wörtl.: vollkommener edler Ritter; Erzählerfigur in den *Canterbury Tales*.
7 **crude:** grob.
mercenary: Söldner.
adulation: Schmeichelei, Lobhudelei.
11 **dewy:** taufeucht, wie Tau.
downy: flaumweich, wie Flaum.
16 **dowdy:** unansehnlich; nachlässig.

older than he, was over fifty. Rain fell off her like water off a duck's back – her skin being oily, not downy. Enid had met Rosanne once or twice baby-sitting; or rather adolescent-sitting, for Walter and Rosanne's two children, Barbara and Bernadette.

Rosanne didn't stand a chance against Enid. Enid still fought the old, old war, and Rosanne had put away her weapons long ago.

"He's so unhappy with his wife," said Enid to Margot. "She's such a cold unfeeling bitch. She's only interested in her career, not in him at all, or the children." Margot was Enid's friend. Margot had owl eyes and a limpid handshake and not a hope of seducing, let alone winning, a married professor. But Margot understood Enid, and was a good friend to her, and had most of the qualities Enid's mother Patty had, and one more important one besides – self-doubt.

"Men never leave their wives for their mistresses," warned Margot. It was a myth much put about, no doubt by wives, in the days of the Great War, to frighten the enemy. Enid knew better: she could tell a savage war mask from the frightened face of a foe in

4 **adolescent-sitting:** Wortschöpfung in Analogie zu *baby-sitting* (*adolescent:* Jugendliche[r], Heranwachsende[r]).
10 **bitch** (coll.): Biest.
12 **owl:** Eule; Eulen-.
limpid: schlaff.
13 **to seduce:** verführen.

retreat. Enid knew Rosanne was frightened by the way she would follow Enid into the kitchen if Walter Walther was there alone, getting ice for drinks or scraping mud from the children's shoes.

Enid was pleased. A frightened foe seldom wins. The attacker is usually victorious, even if the advantage of surprise is gone, especially if the victim is old: Rosanne was old. She'd had the children late. It wasn't as if Walter Walther had really wanted children. He knew what kind of mother she'd make – cold.
Enid was warm. She knew how to silhouette her head against the sunlight so that her hair made a halo round her head, and then turn her face slowly so that the pure line of youth, the one that runs from ear to chin, showed to advantage. Rosanne had trouble with her back. Trouble with her back! Rosanne was a hag with one foot in the grave and with the iron bonds of matrimony would drag Walter Walther down there with her, if Walter didn't somehow break the bonds.

And Enid knew how to behave in bed, too: always keeping something in reserve, never taking the initiative, always the pupil, never the teacher. Enid had seen the *Art of Love* in Rosanne's bookshelves, and guessed her to be sexually experimental and innovatory. And

12 **halo:** Lichterkranz; Heiligenschein.
16 **hag:** hässliches altes Weib, Hexe.
17 **bond:** Fessel.
17 f. **matrimony:** Ehe.
23 **"Art of Love":** englische Übersetzung von *Ars Amatoria* des Ovid.
24 **innovatory:** auf Neuerungen bedacht, erfinderisch.

she was later proved right, when Walter managed to voice one of his few actual complaints about his wife: there was, he felt, something indecent about Rosanne's sexual prowess: something disagreeably insatiable in her desires; it made Walter, from time to humiliating time, impotent.

Otherwise, it wasn't so much lack of love for Rosanne that Walter suffered from, as surfeit of love for Enid.

Enid exulted. And Rosanne was using worn-out old weapons: that particular stage in the war had ended long ago. The battle these days went to the innocent, not to the experienced. Modern man, Enid knew by instinct, especially those with a tendency to impotence, requires docility in bed and admiration and exultation – not excitement and exercise.

"He'll never leave the children," said Margot. "Men don't." But Enid had been left. Enid knew very well that men did. And Barbara and Bernadette were not the most lovable of children – how could they be? With such a mother as Rosanne – a working mother who never even remembered her children's birthdays, never baked a cake, never ironed or darned, never cleaned

4 **prowess:** Verwegenheit.
insatiable: unersättlich.
5 **to humiliate:** demütigen.
8 **surfeit:** Übermaß.
9 **to exult:** jubeln, frohlocken.
14 **docility:** Gelehrigkeit, Fügsamkeit; Sanftmut; Unterwürfigkeit.
exultation: Jubel, Freude.
22 **to darn:** stopfen, flicken.

the oven? Rosanne was a translator with the International Cocoa Board – a genius at languages, but not at motherhood. She was cold, stringy and sour – all the things soft, warm, rounded Enid was not. Walter said so, in bed, and increasingly out of it.

"What are you playing at?" asked Helene, crossly. Her own attitude to the world was moderating. She was an old retired warrior, sitting in a castle she'd won by force of arms, shaking her head at the shockingness of war.

Patty now lived alone in a little council flat in Birmingham. As Enid had left home Arthur no longer paid Patty maintenance. Why should he?

"You want Walter because Walter's Rosanne's," observed Patty to Enid one day in a rare rush of insight to the head. Patty's doctor had started giving her oestrogen for her hot flushes, and side-effects were beginning to show. There was a geranium in a pot on Patty's windowsill, when Enid went to break the news to her mother that Walter was finally leaving Rosanne. A geranium! Patty, who never could see the point in pot plants!

All the same, something, if only oestrogen, was now putting a sparkle in Patty's eye, and she turned up at

3 **stringy:** zäh, sehnig.
10 **council flat:** städtische Wohnung, Sozialwohnung.
15 f. **oestrogen:** Östrogen (weibliches Hormon).
16 **hot flushes:** Hitzewallungen, fliegende Hitze.
17 f. **windowsill:** Fensterbrett, -bank.
23 **sparkle:** Glitzern, Funkeln.

Walter and Enid's wedding in a kind of velvet safari jacket which made her look almost sexy, and when Arthur crossed the room to speak to his ex-wife, she did not turn away, but actually saw the point of shaking his hand, and even laying her cheek against his, in affection and forgiveness.

Enid, in her white velvet trouser suit, saw: and a pang of almost physical pain roared through her, and for a second, just a second, looking at Walter, she saw not her great love but an elderly, paunchy, lecherous stranger. Even though he'd slimmed down quite remarkably during the divorce. It wasn't surprising! Rosanne had behaved like a bitch, and it had told on them both. Nevertheless, people remarked at the wedding that they'd never seen Walter looking so well – or Enid so elegant. He'd somehow scaled down to forty, and she up to thirty. Hardly a difference at all!

Barbara and Bernadette were bridesmaids. Rosanne had been against the idea, out of envy and malice mixed. She hadn't even been prepared to make their dresses, which Enid thought particularly spiteful. "I'd never have made a bridesmaid's dress for you," said

1 **velvet:** Samt.
7 **pang:** Stich.
10 **paunchy:** beleibt, füllig, mit Bauchansatz.
lecherous: lüstern.
13 **to tell on s.o.:** sich bei jdm. zeigen, bemerkbar machen.
16 **to scale down:** hier: sich herunterstufen, verjüngen.
18 **bridesmaid:** Brautjungfer.
19 **malice:** Bosheit.
21 **spiteful:** boshaft, gehässig.

Patty. "Not to wear at your father's wedding." "That's altogether different," said Enid, hurt and confused by the way Patty was seeing the war, almost as if she, Patty, were Rosanne's ally; more Helene's enemy than Enid's mother.

And then Helene upset her. "I hope you're not thinking of having children," she said, during the reception. "Of course I am," said Enid. "Some men can't stand it," said Helene. "Your father, for one. Why do you think I never had any?" "Well, I'm sure he could stand me," said Enid, with a self-confidence she did not feel. For perhaps he just plain couldn't? Perhaps some of the blame for his departure was Enid's, not Patty's. Perhaps if she'd been nicer her father would never have left? And perhaps, indeed, he wouldn't!

Well, if we can't be nice, we can at least try to be perfect. Enid set out on her journey through life with perfection in mind. Doing better! Oh, how neat the corners of the beds she tucked, how fresh the butter, how crisp the tablecloth! Her curtains were always fully lined, her armpits smooth and washed, never merely sprayed. Enid never let her weapons get rusty. She would do better, thank you, than Patty, or Helene, or Rosanne.

Walter Walther clearly adored his Enid and let the world know it. His colleagues half envied, half pitied

12 **plain** (coll., adv.): *plainly.*
19 **to tuck:** feststecken.
20 **crisp:** frisch.

him. Walter would ring Enid from the department twice a day and talk baby-talk at her. Until recently he'd talked to his daughter Barbara in just such a manner. His colleagues came to the conclusion, over many a coffee table, that now the daughter had reached puberty the father, in marrying a girl of roughly the same age, was acting out incest fantasies too terrible to acknowledge. No one mentioned the word love: for this was the new language of the post-war age. If there was to be no hate, how could there be love?

In the meantime, for Walter and Enid, there was perpetual trouble with Rosanne. She insisted at first on staying in the matrimonial home, and it took a lawsuit and some fairly sharp accountants to drive her out: presently she lived with the girls in a little council flat. Oddly enough, it was rather like Patty's. Practical, but somehow depressing. "You see," said Enid. "No gift for living! Poor Walter! What a terrible life she gave him." In the Great War men gave women money, and women gave men life.

Barbara and Bernadette came to stay at weekends. They had their old rooms. Enid prettified them, and lined the curtains. She was a better mother to Barbara and Bernadette than Rosanne had ever been. Walter said so. Enid remembered their birthdays, and saw to their verrucas and had their hair styled. They looked at

13 **matrimonial:** ehelich.
lawsuit: Prozess.
26 **verruca:** Warze.

her with sullen gratitude, like slaves saved from slaughter.

Rosanne lost her job. Rosanne said – of course, it was because the responsibility of being a one-parent family and earning a living was too much for her, but Enid and Walter knew the loss of her job was just a simple matter of redundancy combined with lack of charm. Bernadette's asthma got worse. "Of course the poor child's ill," said Enid. "With such a mother!" Enid didn't believe in truces. She ignored white flags and went in for the kill.

Enid had a pond built in the garden and entertained Walter's friends on Campari and readings of Shakespeare's sonnets. They were literary people, after all, or claimed to be. "Couldn't we do without the sonnets?" said Walter.

But Enid insisted on the sonnets, and the friends drifted away. "It's Rosanne's doing," said Enid. "She's turned them against us." And she twined her white, soft, serpent's arms round his grizzly, stranger body and he believed her. His students, he noticed, seemed less

1 **sullen:** mürrisch.
1 f. **slaughter:** Abschlachten, Gemetzel.
7 **redundancy:** Arbeitslosigkeit; Überfluss, -schuss.
10 **truce:** Waffenstillstand.
10 f. **to go in for the kill:** zum entscheidenden Schlag ausholen.
19 **to twine:** winden, schlingen.
20 **serpent:** Schlange.
grizzly: grau(haarig).

respectful of him than they had been: not as if he had grown younger but they had grown older. Air came through the lecture-room windows, on a hot summer's day, like a sigh. Well, at least he was married, playing honestly and fair, unlike his colleagues, who were for the most part hit-and-run seducers. As for Rosanne, he knew she knew how to look after herself. She always had. A man, in the Great War, usually preferred a woman who couldn't.

"Let's have a baby of our own soon," said Enid. A baby! He hadn't thought of that. She was his baby. Or was he hers?

"We're so happy," said Enid. "You and I. It doesn't matter what the world thinks or says. We were just both a little out of step, that's all, time-wise. God meant us for each other. Don't you feel that?"

He queried her use of the word God, but otherwise agreed with what she said. Her words came as definite instruction from some powerful, knowledgeable source. They flowed, unsullied by doubt. He, being older, had to grope for meanings. He was too wise, and this could only diffuse his certainty, since wisdom is the acknowledgement of ignorance.

6 **hit-and-run seducer:** Mann, der nur darauf aus ist, Frauen im Nu für sich einzunehmen.
15 **to be out of step:** aus dem Schritt, Takt geraten sein.
17 **to query:** in Frage stellen.
20 **unsullied:** (fig.) unbefleckt, unberührt.
21 **to grope for s.th.:** nach etwas suchen.
22 **to diffuse:** (fig.) aufweichen, zerstreuen.

"Of course you should have a baby, Enid," said Patty. "Why not?" But she wasn't really thinking. She was having an affair with a mini-cab driver, and had forgotten about Enid. "Your behaviour is obscene and disgusting," Enid shouted at her mother. "*He's young.*" "What's the point in your making all this fuss?" asked Patty. "I deserve a little happiness in my life, and I'm sure you brought me precious little!"

Enid got pregnant, straight away. Walter went out and got drunk when he heard, with old friends of himself and Rosanne. Enid was so upset by this double disloyalty she went and stayed with her friend Margot for at least three days.

Margot was married and pregnant, too, and by one of Walter Walther's students, who had spots and bad breath. They lived on their grants, and beans and cider. Nevertheless, her husband went with her to the antenatal clinic and they pored over baby books together. Walter Walther took the view, common in the Great War, that the begetting of children was something to do

4 **obscene:** unanständig, widerlich.
8 **precious little** (coll.): herzlich wenig.
9 **pregnant:** schwanger.
11 f. **disloyalty:** Untreue.
15 **spots** (pl.): Pickel.
16 **grant:** Stipendium.
cider: Cidre, Apfelwein.
17 f. **antenatal clinic:** Klinik für werdende Mütter.
18 **to pore over s.th.:** etwas genau studieren.
20 **begetting:** Zeugung.

with the one-upmanship of woman against woman, and very little to do with the man.

"Look, Enid," said Walter, a new Walter, briskly and unkindly, "you just get on with it by yourself." Arthur had left Patty to get on with it by herself, too. Her very name, Enid, had been a last-minute choice by Patty with the registrar hovering over her hospital bed, because Arthur just left it to her.

"You can't have everything," was what Helene said, when Enid murmured a complaint or two. "You can't have status, money, adoration and what Margot has as well."

"Why not?" demanded Enid. "I want *everything*!"

Enid saw herself on a mountain top, a million women bowing down before her, acknowledging her victory. Her foot would be heavy on the necks of those she humbled. That was how it ought to be. She pulled herself together. She knew that, in the Great War, being pregnant could make you or break you. Great prizes were to be won – the best mother, the prettiest child, the whitest white – but much was risked. The enemy could swoop down, slender-waisted and laughing and

1 **one-upmanship:** Konkurrenzverhalten.
3 **briskly** (adv.): forsch.
7 **registrar:** Standesbeamter.
to hover over s.th.: um etwas herumstreifen, bei etwas herumstehen.
17 **to humble:** übertrumpfen, ausstechen.
22 **to swoop down:** zustoßen, zum Angriff ausholen.

lively, and deliver any number of mortal wounds. So Enid wore her prettiest clothes, and sighed a little but never grunted when the baby lay on some pelvic nerve or other, and never let Walter suffer a moment because of what he had done to her. (In those pre-pill days men made women pregnant: women didn't just get pregnant.)

His boiled egg and toast soldiers and freshly milled coffee and the single flower in the silver vase were always there on the breakfast table at half past eight sharp and they'd eat together, companionably. Rosanne had slopped Sugar Puffs into bowls for the family breakfast, and they'd eaten among the uncleared children's homework and students' essays. Slut!

Walter was protective. "We have to take extra special care of you," he'd say, helping her across roads. But he seemed a little embarrassed. Something grated: she didn't know what. They ate in rather more often than before.

Then Rosanne, who ought by rights to have been lying punch-drunk in some obscure corner of the battlefield, rose up and delivered a nasty body-blow. Barbara and Bernadette were to come to live with Enid and Walter.

3 **to grunt:** stöhnen.
pelvic: Becken-.
8 **toast soldier:** etwa: Toaststreifen.
12 **to slop:** kippen, schütten, klatschen.
14 **slut:** Schlampe.
17 **to grate:** kratzen, knirschen, reiben, mahlen.
21 **punch-drunk:** sturzbetrunken.
obscure: dunkel.

Rosanne couldn't cope, in such crowded surroundings. She had a new job, and couldn't always be rushing home for Bernadette's asthma. Could she?

"A new boyfriend, more like," said Walter, bitterly. Enid restrained from pointing out that Rosanne was an old, old woman with a bad back and hardly in the field for admirers.

Now six perfectly cooked boiled eggs on the table each morning – Bernadette and Barbara demanded two each – is twelve times as difficult to achieve as two. By the time the last one's in, the first one's cooked, but which one is it?

Walter looked at his bowl of Sugar Puffs one morning and said, "Just like old times," and the girls looked knowingly and giggled. They looked at Enid and her swelling tum with contempt and pity. They borrowed her clothes and her make-up. They refused to be taken to art galleries, or theatres; they refused even to play Monopoly, let alone Happy Families. They referred to their father as the Old Goat.

Sometimes she hated them. But Walter would not let her. "Look," said Walter, "you did come along and disrupt their lives. You owe them something, at least." As

1 **to cope:** zurecht-, klarkommen.
15 **to giggle:** kichern.
16 **tum:** Bauch.
22 f. **to disrupt:** aus den Fugen geraten lassen.

if it was all nothing to do with him. Which in a way it wasn't. It was between Rosanne and Enid.

Enid locked herself out of the house one day and, though she knew the girls were inside, when she knocked they wouldn't let her in. It was raining. Afterwards they just said they hadn't heard. And she'd fallen and hurt her knee trying to climb in the window, and might have lost the baby. Bernadette threw a bad asthma attack and got all the attention.

Walter spent more and more time in the department. She and he hardly made love at all any more. It didn't seem right.

Enid went into labour at eight o'clock one evening. She rang Walter Walther at the English Department where he said he was, but he wasn't. She rang Margot and wept, and Margot said, "I don't think I've ever known you cry, Enid," and Margot's spotty husband said, "You'll probably find him round at Rosanne's. I wouldn't tell you, if it wasn't an emergency."

"Yes," said Barbara and Bernadette. "He goes round to see Mum quite a lot. We didn't like to tell you because we didn't want to upset you.

"Really," they said, "the whole thing was a plot to get rid of us. The thing is, neither of them can stand us." (Barbara and Bernadette went to one of the large new comprehensive schools, where there were pupil-coun-

26 f. **pupil-counseller:** Schülerberater(in), Vertrauensschüler(in).

sellors, who could explain everything and anything, and were never lost for words.)

Enid screamed and wept all through her labour, not just from pain. They'd never known a noisier mother, they said: and she'd been so quiet and elegant and self-controlled throughout her pregnancy.

Enid gave birth to a little girl. Now in the Great War, the birth of a girl was, understandably, and unlike now, cause for commiseration rather than rejoicing. Nevertheless, Enid rejoiced. And in so doing, abandoned a battle which was really none of her making; she laid down her arms: she kissed her mother and Helene when they came to visit her, clasped her baby and admitted weakness and distress to Barbara and Bernadette, who actually then seemed quite to like her.

Walter Walther did not come home. He stayed with Rosanne. Enid, Barbara and Bernadette lived in the same house, shared suspender belts, shampoo and boyfriends, and looked after baby Belinda. Walter and Rosanne visited, sheepishly, from time to time, and sent money. Enid went back to college and took a degree in psychology, and was later to earn a good living as a research scientist.

9 **commiseration:** Mitleid.
rejoicing: Freude, Jubel.
18 **suspender belt:** Strumpfbandgürtel.
20 **sheepishly** (adv.): verlegen, kleinlaut.

Later still she was to become something of a propagandist in the new cold war against men; she wore jeans and a donkey jacket and walked round linked arm-in-arm with women. But that was, perhaps, hardly surprising, so treacherous had the old male allies turned out to be. All the same, yesterday's enemy, tomorrow's friend! Who is to say what will happen next?

3 **donkey jacket:** dicke, wasserundurchlässige Jacke, Parka.
5 **treacherous:** verräterisch.

Sara Maitland

The Wicked Stepmother's Tale

The wife of a rich man fell sick and as she felt that her end was drawing near, she called her only daughter to her bedside and said, "Dear Child, be good and pious, and then the good God will always protect you, and I will look down from heaven and be near you." Thereupon she closed her eyes and departed. Every day the maiden went out to her mother's grave and wept, and she remained pious and good. When winter came the snow spread a white sheet over the grave and by the time the spring sun had drawn it off again the man had taken another wife …

Now began a bad time for the poor stepchild … They took her pretty clothes away, put an old grey bedgown on her and gave her wooden shoes … She had to do hard work from morning to night, get up before daybreak, carry water, light fires, cook and wash … In the evening when she had worked until she was weary she had no bed to go to, but had to sleep by the hearth in the cinders. And as on that ac-

2 **stepmother:** Stiefmutter.
6 **pious:** fromm.
8 **to depart:** dahinscheiden, versterben.
16 **bedgown:** Nachthemd.
21 **hearth:** Feuerstelle, Herd.
cinders (pl.): Asche.

count she always looked dusty and dirty, they called her Cinderella.

You know the rest I expect. Almost everyone does.

I'm not exactly looking for self-justification. There's this thing going on at the moment where women tell all the old stories again and turn them inside-out and back-to-front – so the characters you always thought were the goodies turn out to be the baddies, and vice versa, and whole lot of guilt is laid to rest: or that at least is the theory. I'm not sure myself that the guilt isn't just passed on to the next person, *intacta* so to speak. Certainly I want to carry and cope with my own guilt, because I want to carry and cope with my own virtue and I really don't see that you can have one without the other. Anyway it would be hard to find a version of this story where I would come out a shiny new-style heroine: no true version anyway. All I want to say is that it's more complicated, more complex, than it's told, and the reasons why it's told the way it is are complex too.

But I'm not willing to be a victim. I was not innocent, and I have grown out of innocence now and even out of wanting to be thought innocent. Living is a harsh busi-

4 **self-justification:** Selbstrechtfertigung, -gerechtigkeit.
8 **the goodies / the baddies** (coll.): die Guten, die Bösen.
8 f. **vice versa:** umgekehrt.
9 **to lay s.th. to rest:** (fig.) etwas begraben.
11 **intactus, a, um** (Lat.): intakt, unversehrt, unangetastet, ungeschmälert.
12 **to cope with s.th.:** mit etwas klarkommen, etwas bewältigen.
23 **harsh:** (fig.) hart, rauh.

ness, as no one warned us when we were young and carefree under the apple bough, and I feel the weight of that ancient harshness and I want to embrace it, and not opt for some washed-out aseptic, hand wringing, Disneyland garbage. (Though come to think of it he went none-too-easy on stepmothers did he? Snow White scared the socks off me the first time I saw the film – and partly of course because I recognised myself. But I digress.)

Look. It was like this. Or rather it was more like this, or parts of it were like this, or this is one part of it.

She was dead pretty in a Pears Soap sort of way, and, honestly, terribly sweet and good. At first all I wanted her to do was concentrate. Concentration is the key to power. You have to concentrate on what is real. Concentration is not good or bad necessarily, but it is powerful. Enough power to change the world, that's all I wanted. (I was younger then, of course; but actually they're starving and killing whales and forests and each other out there; shutting your eyes and pretending

2 **apple bough:** Apfelbaumzweig.
4 **to opt for s.th.:** sich für etwas entscheiden, etwas wählen.
washed-out: (fig.) verwaschen, abgedroschen.
aseptic: aseptisch, keimfrei.
5 **he:** Gemeint ist Walt Disney.
6 **to go on s.o.:** über jdn. herziehen.
none-too-easy (coll.): nicht gerade sanft.
6 f. **Snow White:** Schneewittchen.
7 **to scare the socks off s.o.:** jdm. furchtbar Angst einjagen.
9 **to digress:** abschweifen.
12 **Pears Soap:** bekannte Seifenmarke; hier: Anspielung auf einen Reklamespruch.

they're not doesn't change anything. It does matter.) And what she was not was powerful. She wouldn't look out for herself. She was so sweet and so hopeful; so full of faith and forgiveness and love. You have to touch anger somewhere, rage even; you have to spit and roar and bite and scream and know it before you can be safe. And she never bloody would.

When I first married her father I thought she was so lovely, so good and so sad. And so like her mother. I knew her mother very well, you see; we grew up together. I loved her mother. Really. With so much hope and fondness and awareness of her worth. But – and I don't know how to explain this without sounding like an embittered old bitch which I probably am – she was too good. Too giving. She gave herself away, indiscriminately. She didn't even give herself as a precious gift. She gave herself away as though she wasn't worth hanging on to. Generous to a fault, they said when she was young, but no one acted as though it were a fault, so she never learned. "Free with Kellogg's Cornflakes" was her motto. She equated loving with suffering I thought at one time, but that wasn't right, it was worse, she equated loving with being; as though she did not exist unless she was denying her existence. I mean, he

12 **fondness:** Zärtlichkeit; Liebenswürdigkeit.
14 **embittered:** verbittert.
bitch (coll.): Biest.
15 f. **indiscriminately** (adv.): unkritisch, wahllos, unüberlegt.
18 **to a fault:** im Übermaß, übermäßig.
20 **Free with Kellogg's Cornflakes:** Reklamespruch, der für Werbegeschenke der Firma Kellogg's kreiert wurde.
21 **to equate:** gleichstellen, -setzen.

was not a bad bloke her husband, indeed I'm married to him myself, and I like him and we have good times together, but he wasn't worth it – no one is – not what she gave him, which was her whole self with no price tag on.

And it was just the same with that child. Yes, yes one can understand: she had difficulty getting pregnant actually, she had difficulties carrying those babies to term too. Even I can guess how that might hurt. But her little girl was her great reward for suffering, and at the same time was also her handle on a whole new world of self-giving. And yes, of course she looked so lovely, who could have resisted her, propped up in her bed with that tiny lovely child sucking, sucking, sucking; the mother who denied her little one nothing, the good mother, the one we all longed for, pouring herself out into the child. Well, I'll tell you, I've done it too, it is hell caring for a tiny daughter, I know. Everything, everything drags you into hell: the fact that you love and desire her, the fact that she's so needy and vulnerable, the fact that she never leaves you alone until your dreams are smashed in little piles and shabby with neglect, the fact that pleasure and guilt come so precisely together, as so seldom happens, working towards the same end and sucking your very selfhood out of you. It

1 **bloke** (slang): Kerl.
4 f. **price tag:** Preisschild.
7 **pregnant:** schwanger.
8 **to carry a baby to term:** ein Kind, eine Schwangerschaft austragen.
13 (*to be*) **propped up:** (mit dem Rücken an etwas gelehnt) sitzen, sich lehnen.
20 **needy:** bedürftig.

is a perilous time for a woman, that nursing of a daughter, and you can only survive it if you cling to yourself with a fierce and passionate love, *and* you back that up with a trained and militant lust for justice *and* you scream to the people around you to meet your needs and desires *and* you do not let them off, *and* when all is said and done you sit back and laugh at yourself with a well timed and not unmalicious irony. Well she could not, of course she could not, so she did not survive. She was never angry, she never asked, she took resignation – that tragic so-called virtue – as a ninth-rate alternative to reality and never even realised she had been short-changed.

So when I first married my husband I only meant to tease her a little, to rile her, to make her fight back. I couldn't bear it, that she was so like her mother and would go the same way. My girls were more like me, less agreeable to have about the house, but tough as old boots and capable of getting what they needed and not worrying too much about what they wanted or oughted, so to speak. I didn't have to worry about them. I just could not believe the sweetness of that little girl and her wide-eyed belief that I would be happy and love her if she would just deny herself and follow

1 **perilous:** gefährlich.
3 **to back s.th. up:** etwas unterstützen.
8 **unmalicious:** frei von Häme.
11 **ninth-rate:** neuntklassig, d. h. schäbig.
12 f. **to be short-changed** (coll.): übers Ohr gehauen werden.
15 **to tease:** necken, foppen.
to rile: ärgern.
21 **to ought** (arch.): (etwas) schuldig sein.

me. So of course I exploited her a bit, pushed and tested it, if you understand, because I couldn't believe it. Then I just wanted her to *see*, to see that life is not all sweetness and light, that people are not automatically to be trusted, that fairy-godmothers are unreliable and damned thin on the ground, and that even the most silvery of princes soon go out hunting and fighting and drinking and whoring, and don't give one tuppeny ha'penny curse more for you than you give for yourself. Well she could have looked at her father and known. He hardly proved himself to be the great romantic lover of all time, even at an age when that would have been appropriate, never mind later. He had replaced darling Mummy with me, after all, and pretty damned quick too, and so long as he was getting his end off and his supper on the table he wasn't going to exert himself on her behalf, as I pointed out to her, by no means kindly.

(And, I should like to add, I still don't understand about that. I couldn't believe how little the bastard finally cared when it came to the point. Perhaps he was bored to tears by goodness, perhaps he was too lazy. He was a sentimental old fart about her of course, his

1 **to exploit:** ausbeuten.
5 **fairy-godmother:** gute Fee.
6 **to be thin on the ground:** (fig.) dünn gesät sein.
8 **to whore:** herumhuren.
8f. **one tupenny ha'penny** (coll.): etwa: keine müde Mark.
15 **to get one's end off** (coll.): sein(en), ihr(en) Teil weghaben, abbekommen.
20 **bastard** (slang): Schuft.
23 **old fart** (slang): etwa: alter Stinker, Scheißer (*fart:* Furz).

eyes could fill with nostalgic tears every time he looked at her and thought of her dead mother; but he never *did* anything; or even asked me to stop doing anything. She never asked, and he never had eyes to see, or energy or ... God knows what went on his head about her and as far as I'm concerned God's welcome. She loved him and trusted him and served him and he never even bloody noticed. Which sort of makes my point actually because he would never treat me like that, and yet he and I get on very well now; like each other and have good times in bed and out of it. Of course I'd never have let him tell me how to behave, but he might have tried, at least just once.)

Anyway, no, she would not see. She would not blame her father. She would not blame her mother, not even for dying, which is the ultimate outrage from someone you love. And she would not blame me. She just smiled and accepted, smiled and invented castles in the air to which someone, though not herself, would come and take her one day, smiled and loved me. No matter what I did to her, she just smiled.

So, yes, in the end I was cruel. I don't know how to explain it and I do not attempt to justify it. Her wetness *infuriated* me. I could not shake her good will, her hopefulness, her capacity to love and love such a point-

1 **nostalgic:** nostalgisch, sehnsüchtig, wehmütig.
16 **outrage:** Frevel, Missetat.
23 **wetness:** etwa: Widerstandslosigkeit (*wet* [slang]: schlapp[schwänzig]).
24 **to infuriate:** in Rage versetzen.
25 f. **pointless:** sinnlos.

less and even dangerous object. I could not make her hate me. Not even for a moment. I could not make her hate me. And I cannot explain what that frustration did to me. I hated her insane dog-like devotion where it was so undeserved. She treated me as her mother had treated him. I think I hated her stupidity most of all. I can hear myself almost blaming her for my belly deep madness; I don't want to do that; I don't want to get into blaming the victim and she was my victim. I was older than her, and stronger than her, and had more power than her; and there was no excuse. No excuse, I thought the first time I ever hit her, but there was an excuse and it was my wild need, and it escalated.

So in the end – and yes I have examined all the motives and reasons why one woman should be cruel to another and I do not find them explanatory – so in the end I was cruel to her. I goaded and humiliated and pushed and bullied her. I used all my powers, my superior strength, my superior age, my superior intelligence against her. I beat her, in the end, systematically and severely; but more than that I used her and worked her and denied her pleasures and gave her pain. I violated

4 **insane:** verrückt, wahnsinnig.
devotion: Hingabe.
7 f. **belly deep madness:** etwa: eingefleischte Wut.
13 **to escalate:** eskalieren, sich steigern.
16 **explanatory:** einleuchtend, hinreichend klar.
17 **to goad:** antreiben, aufstacheln, reizen.
to humiliate: demütigen.
18 **to bully:** schikanieren, tyrannisieren.
21 **to work s.o.:** jdn. hart herannehmen.
22 **to violate s.th.:** etwas verletzen, stören; gegen etwas verstoßen.

her space, her dignity, her integrity, her privacy, even her humanity and perhaps her physical safety. There was an insane urge in me, not simply to hurt her, but to have her admit that I had hurt her. I would lie awake at night appalled, and scald myself with contempt, with anger and with self-disgust, but I had only to see her in the morning for my temper to rise and I would start again, start again at her with an unreasonable savagery that seemed to upset me more than it upset her. Picking, picking and pecking, endlessly. She tried my patience as no one else had ever done and finally I gave up the struggle and threw it away and entered into the horrible game with all my considerable capacity for concentration.

And nothing worked. I could not make her angry. I could not make her hate me. I could not stop her loving me with a depth and a generosity and a forgiveness that were the final blow. Nothing moved her to more than a simper. Nothing penetrated the fantasies and day-dreams with which her head was stuffed so full I'm surprised she didn't slur her consonants. She was

1 **space:** Bewegungsfreiheit, (individuelle) Grenzen.
privacy: Privatleben.
5 **appalled:** entsetzt.
to scald: hier: (fig.) sich verbrühen, innerlich verzehren.
6 **self-disgust:** Selbstverachtung.
7 **temper:** Zorn, Unmut.
8 **savagery:** Wildheit, Rohheit.
10 **to peck:** (auf jdm. herum)hacken.
to try s.th.: etwas auf die Probe stellen.
19 **simper:** einfältiges Lächeln.
20 **stuffed:** vollgestopft.
21 **to slur:** undeutlich aussprechen.

locked into perpetual passivity and gratitude and love. Even when she was beaten she covered her bruises to protect me; even when she was hungry she would not take food from my cupboards to feed herself; even when I mocked her she smiled at me tenderly.

All I wanted was for her to grow up, to grow up and realise that life was not a bed of roses and that she had to take some responsibility for her own life, to take some action on her own behalf, instead of waiting and waiting and waiting for something or someone to come shining out of the dark and force safety on her as I forced pain. What Someone? Another like her father who had done nothing, nothing whatever, to help her and never would? Another like him whom she could love generously and hopelessly and serve touchingly and givingly until weariness and pain killed her too. I couldn't stand it. Even when I beat her, even as I beat her, she loved me, she just loved and smiled and hoped and waited, day-dreamed and night-dreamed, and waited and waited and waited. She was untouchable and infantile. I couldn't save her and I couldn't damage her. God knows, I tried.

Now of course it's just an ancient habit. It has lost its sharp edges, lost the passion in both of us to see it out in conflict, between dream and reality, between hope and cynicism. There is a great weariness in me, and I

1 **perpetual:** ständig.
2 **bruise:** blauer Fleck, Prellung.
5 **to mock s.o.:** jdn. verspotten, sich über jdn.lustig machen.
21 **infantile:** infantil, kindlich; kindisch.
26 **cynicism:** Zynismus, Spott, Hohn.

cannot summon up the fire of conviction. I do not concentrate any more. I do not have enough concentration, enough energy, enough power. Perhaps she has won, because she drained that out of me years and years ago. Sometimes I despair, which wastes still more concentration. We plod on together, because we always have. Sweetly she keeps at it, smile, smile, dream, hope, wait, love, forgive, smile, smile, bloody smile. Tiredly, I keep at it too: "Sweep that grate." "Tidy your room." "Do your homework." "What can you see in that nerd." "Take out those damn ear-phones and pay attention." "Life doesn't come free, you have to work on it." "Wake up, hurry up, stop day-dreaming, no you can't, yes you must, get a move on, don't be so stupid." And "You're not going to the Ball, or party, or disco, or over to your Nan's, dressed like *that*."

She calls it nagging.

She calls me Mummy.

1 **to summon up:** (fig.) wecken, aufbringen.
4 **to drain s.th. out:** etwas abzapfen.
6 **to plod on:** sich vorwärtsmühen, weiterkämpfen.
9 **grate:** Kamin, Feuerrost.
11 **nerd** (slang): doofe, blöde Person.
ear-phones (pl.): Kopfhörer.
14 **get a move on** (coll.): beweg dich!, mach voran!
16 **nan:** Kurzform für *nanny:* Omi (Kindersprache).
17 **to nag:** nörgeln.

Penelope Fitzgerald

At Hiruharama

Mr Tanner was anxious to explain how it was that he had a lawyer in the family, so that when they all decided to sell up and quit New Zealand there had been someone they could absolutely trust with the legal business. That meant that he had to say something about his grandfather, who had been an orphan from Stamford in Lincolnshire and was sent out to a well-to-do family north of Auckland, supposedly as an apprentice, but it turned out that he was to be more or less of a servant. He cleaned the knives, saw to the horses, waited at table and chopped the wood. On an errand to a dry goods store in Auckland he met Kitty, Mr Tanner's grandmother. She had come out from England as a governess, and she too found she was really wanted as a servant. She was sixteen, and Tanner asked her to wait for three years while he saved his wages, and then to marry him. All this was at a Methodist social, say a

8 **orphan:** Waisenkind.
9 **Lincolnshire:** Grafschaft in Mittelengland.
10 **Auckland:** neuseeländische Stadt im Norden der Nordinsel.
13 **errand:** Botengang, Besorgung.
13 f. **dry goods**: Textilien, Meterware.
16 **governess:** Gouvernante.
19 **Methodist social:** Methodistenabend, -versammlung, -treffen.
say (coll.): etwa.

couple of weeks later. "What family have you got back home?" Kitty asked him. Tanner replied just the one sister. Younger or older? Older. She probably thinks I'm a skilled craftsman by now. She probably reckons I'm made. – Haven't you sent word to her lately? – Not lately. – Best write to her now, anyway, said Kitty, and tell her how it is between us. I should be glad to have a new relation, I haven't many – I'll think it over, he said. Kitty realised then that he could neither read nor write.

They had to start in a remote country place. The land round Auckland at that time was ten shillings an acre, a third of the price going to build the new churches and schools, but where Tanner and Kitty went, north of Awanui, there weren't any churches and schools, and it was considerably cheaper. They didn't have to buy their place, it had been left deserted, and yet it had something you could give a thousand pounds for and not get, and that was a standpipe giving constant clear water from an underground well. But whoever lived there had given up, because of the loneliness and because it was such poor country. Don't picture a shack, though. There were two rooms, one with a stove and one with a bedstead, and a third one at the back for a vegetable store. Tanner grew root vegetables and went into Awa-

4 **craftsman:** Handwerker.
5 **to be made:** etwa: ein gemachter Mann sein, es geschafft haben.
12 **acre:** Flächenmaß; entspricht etwa 4047 m^2.
19 **standpipe:** Standrohr.
22 **shack:** Schuppen, Hütte.
24 **bedstead:** Bettstatt.

nui twice a week with the horse and dray. Kitty stayed behind, because they'd taken on two hundred chickens and a good few pigs.

Tanner turned over in his mind what he'd say to his wife when she told him she was going to have a child. When she did tell him, which wasn't for another two years or so, by the way, he didn't hear her at first, because a northerly was blowing and neither of them could expect to hear each other. When he did catch what she was saying, he hitched up and drove into Awanui. The doctor was at his midday dinner, which he took at a boarding-house higher up the main street. When he got back and into his consulting-room Tanner asked him what were the life statistics of the North Island.

"Do you mean the death statistics?" the doctor asked.

"They'll do just as well," said Tanner.

"No one dies here except from drink or drowning. Out of three thousand people in Taranaki Province there hasn't been a single funeral in the last sixteen months and only twenty-four sick and infirm. You may look upon me as a poor man."

"What about women in childbirth?" asked Tanner.

The doctor didn't have any figures for women dying in

1 **dray:** Pferdewagen, Karren.
8 **northerly:** Nordwind.
10 **to hitch up:** (Pferde) anspannen.
12 **boarding-house:** Pension.
22 **infirm:** gebrechlich.
24 **childbirth:** Geburt, Kindbett.

childbirth, but he looked sharply at Tanner and asked him when his child was due.

"You don't know, of course. Well, don't ask me if it's going to be twins. Nature didn't intend us to know that." He began to write in his notebook. "Where are you living?"

"It's off the road to Houhora, you turn off to the right after twelve miles."

"What's it called?"

"Hiruharama."

"Don't know it. That's not a Maori name."

"I think it means Jerusalem," said Tanner.

"Are there any other women about the place?"

"No."

"I mean someone who could come in and look after things while your wife's laid up. Who's your nearest neighbour?" Tanner told him there was no one except a man called Brinkman, who came over sometimes. He was about nine or ten miles off at Stony Loaf.

"And he has a wife?"

"No, he hasn't, that's what he complains about. You couldn't ask a woman to live out there."

"You can ask a woman to live anywhere," said the doctor. "He's a crank, I dare say."

"He's a dreamer," Tanner replied. "I should term Brinkman a dreamer."

"I was thinking in terms of washing the sheets, that sort of thing. If there's no one else, can you manage about the house yourself for a few days?"

11 **Maori:** ursprüngliche Einwohner Neuseelands.
24 **crank:** komischer Kauz.

"I can do anything about the house," said Tanner.

"You don't drink?"

Tanner shook his head, wondering if the doctor did. He asked if he shouldn't bring his wife with him for a consultation next time he drove over to Awanui. The doctor looked out of his window at the bone-shaking old dray with its iron-rimmed wheels. "Don't."

He tore the prescription out of his notebook. "Get this for your wife. It's calcium water. When you want me to come, you'll have to send for me. But don't let that worry you. Often by the time I arrive I'm not needed."

Other patients had arrived and were sitting on the wooden benches on the verandah. Some had empty medicine bottles for a refill. There was a man with his right arm strapped up, several kids with their mothers, and a woman who looked well enough but seemed to be in tears for some reason or other. – Well, you see life in the townships.

Tanner went over to the post office, where there was free pen and ink if you wanted it, and wrote a letter to his sister. – But wait a minute, surely he couldn't read or write? Evidently by that time he could. Mr Tanner's guess was that although Kitty was a quiet girl, very quiet, she'd refused to marry him until he'd got the hang of it. – Tanner wrote: My darling old sister. Well,

6 **bone-shaking:** Adjektiv zu *bone-shaker:* Klapperkiste, Knochenmühle.

7 **iron-rimmed:** mit Eisenfelgen.

16 **to strap s.th. up:** etwas hochbinden.

25 f. **to get the hang of s.th.:** etwas kapieren, den Dreh von etwas herausbekommen, mit etwas klarkommen.

it's come to pass and either a girl or a boy will be added unto us. It would be a help if you could send us a book on the subject. We have now a hundred full-grown hens and a further hundred at point of lay, and a good stand of potatoes. – After mailing the letter he bought soap, thread, needles, canned fish, tea and sugar. When he drove out of Awanui he stopped at the last homestead, where he knew a man called Parrish who kept racing-pigeons. Some of them, in fact were just arriving back at their loft. Parrish had cut the entrances to the nests down very small, and every time a bird got home it had to squeeze past a bell on a string so that the tinkling sound gave warning. They were all Blue Chequers, the only kind, Parrish declared, that a sane man would want to keep. Tanner explained his predicament and asked for the loan of two birds. Parrish didn't mind, because Hiruharama, Tanner's place, was on a more or less direct line from Awanui to Te Paki station, and that was the line his pigeons flew.

"If you'd have lived over the other way I couldn't have helped you," Parrish said.

A Maori boy took the young birds out as soon as they were four months old and tossed them at three miles,

1 **it's come to pass:** etwa: es ist nun so weit.
4 **at point of lay:** legereif.
stand: Bestand.
7 **homestead:** Haus, Heim.
8 f. **racing-pigeon:** Brieftaube.
10 **loft:** (Tauben-)Schlag.
12 **to tinkle:** klingeln.
14 **sane:** geistig gesund, vernünftig.
15 **predicament:** schwierige Lage.
23 **to toss:** (in die Luft) werfen, loslassen, -schicken.

ten miles, twenty miles, always in the same direction, north-north-west of Awanui.

“As long as they can do fifteen miles,” said Tanner. “They can do two hundred and fifty.”

“How long will it take them to do fifteen miles?”

“Twenty minutes in clear weather,” said Parrish.

The Maori boy chose out two birds and packed them into a wicker hamper, which Tanner wedged into the driver’s seat of the dray.

“Have you got them numbered in some way?” Tanner asked.

“I don’t need to. I know them all,” said Parrish.

He added that they would need rock salt, so Tanner drove back into the town once more to buy the rock salt and a sack of millet. By the time he got to Hiruharama the dark clear night sky was pressing in on every side. I ought to have taken you with me, he told Kitty. She said she had been all right. He hadn’t, though, he’d been worried. You mean you’ve forgotten something at the stores, said Kitty. Tanner went out to the dray and fetched the pigeons, still shifting about and conferring quietly in their wicker basket.

“Here’s one thing more than you asked for,” he said. They found room for them in the loft above the vegetable store. The Blue Chequers were the prettiest things about the place.

The sister in England did send a book, although it

8 **wicker hamper:** Weidekorb.
to wedge: zwängen.
13 **rock salt:** Steinsalz, grobes Salz.
15 **millet:** Hirse.
21 **to confer:** sich austauschen, unterhalten.

didn't arrive for almost a year. In any case, it only had one chapter of a practical nature. Otherwise, it was religious in tone. But meanwhile Kitty's calculations couldn't have been far out, because more or less when they expected it the pains came on strong enough for Tanner to send for the doctor.

He had made the pigeon's nests out of packing-cases. They ought to have flown out daily for exercise, but he hadn't been able to manage that. Still, they looked fair enough, a bit dishevelled, but not so that you'd notice. It was four o'clock, breezy, but not windy. He took them out into the bright air which, even that far from the coast, was full of the salt of the ocean. How to toss a pigeon he had no idea. He opened the basket, and before he could think what to do next they were out and up into the blue. He watched in terror as after reaching a certain height they began turning round in tight circles as though puzzled or lost. Then, apparently sighting something on the horizon that they knew, they set off strongly towards Awanui. – Say twenty minutes for them to get to Parrish's loft. Ten minutes for Parrish or the Maori boy to walk up the street to the doctor's. Two and a half hours for the doctor to drive over, even allowing for his losing the way once. Thirty seconds for him to get down from his trap and open his bag. –

At five o'clock Tanner went out to see to the pigs and

5 **pains:** hier: Geburtswehen.
10 **dishevelled:** zerzaust.
11 **breezy:** (leicht) windig.
25 **trap:** Einspänner.

hens. At six Kitty was no better and no worse. She lay there quietly, sweating from head to foot. "I can hear someone coming," she said, not from Awanui, though, it was along the top road. Tanner thought it must be Brinkman. "Why, yes, it must be six months since he came," said Kitty, as though she was making conversation. Who else, after all, could it have been on the top road? The track up there had a deep rounded gutter each side which made it awkward to drive along. They could hear the screeching and rattling of his old buggy, two wheels in the gutter, two out. "He's stopped at the gully now to let his horse drink," said Kitty. "He'll have to let it walk the rest of the way." – "He'll have to turn round when he gets here and start right back," said Tanner.

There used to be a photograph of Brinkman somewhere, but Mr Tanner didn't know what had become of it, and he believed it hadn't been a good likeness in any case. – Of course, in the circumstances, as he'd come eight miles over a rough road, he had to be asked to put up his horse for a while, and come in.

Like most people who live on their own Brinkman continued with the course of his thoughts, which were more real to him than the outside world's commotion. Walking straight into the front room he stopped in

8 **gutter:** Gosse, Rinnstein.
10 **screeching:** Quietschen.
rattling: Klappern.
buggy: einspänniger, ungedeckter Pferdewagen.
12 **gully:** Abzugs-, Entwässerungsrinne.
24 **commotion:** Bewegung, Aufruhr, Tumult.

front of the piece of mirror-glass tacked over the sink and looked fixedly into it.

"I'll tell you something, Tanner, I thought I caught sight of my first grey hairs this morning."

"I'm sorry to hear that."

Brinkman looked round. "I see the table isn't set."

"I don't want you to feel that you're not welcome," said Tanner, "but Kitty's not well. She told me to be sure that you came in and rested a while, but she's not well. Truth is, she's in labour."

"Then she won't be cooking dinner this evening, then?"

"You mean you were counting on having it here?"

"My half-yearly dinner with you and Mrs Tanner, yis, that's about it."

"What day is it, then?" asked Tanner, somewhat at random. It was almost too much for him at that moment to realise that Brinkman existed. He seemed like a stranger, perhaps from a foreign country, not understanding how ordinary things were done or said.

Brinkman made no attempt to leave, but said; "Last time I came here we started with canned toheroas. Your wife set them in front of me. I'm not sure that they had an entirely good effect on the intestines. Then we had fried eggs and excellent jellied beetroot, a choice between tea or Bovo, bread and butter and un-

1 **to tack:** heften, befestigen.
22 **toheroas** (pl.): neuseeländische Muschelart.
24 **intestines:** Eingeweide, Verdauungsorgane.
25 **jellied:** geliert.
beetroot: rote Rüben, Rote Bete.
26 **Bovo:** Handelsname für eine Rinderbouillon.

limited quantities of treacle. I have a note of all this in my daily journal. That's not to say, however, that I came over here simply to take dinner with you. It wasn't for the drive, either, although I'm always glad to have the opportunity of a change of scene and to read a little in Nature's book. No, I've come today, as I came formerly, for the sake of hearing a woman's voice."

Had Tanner noticed, he went on, that there were no native songbirds in the territory? At that moment there was a crying, or a calling, from the next room such as Tanner had never heard before, not in a shipwreck – and he had been in a wreck – not in a slaughterhouse.

"Don't put yourself out on my account," said Brinkman. "I'm going to sit here until you come back and have a quiet smoko."

The doctor drove up bringing with him his wife's widowed sister, who lived with them and was a nurse, or had been a nurse. Tanner came out of the bedroom covered with blood, something like a butcher. He told the doctor he'd managed to deliver the child, a girl, in fact he'd wrapped it in a towel and tucked it up in the washbasket. The doctor took him back into the bedroom and made him sit down. The nurse put down the things she'd brought with her and looked round for the

1 **treacle:** Sirup, Melasse.
11 **shipwreck:** Schiffbruch.
12 f. **slaughterhouse:** Schlachthof.
14 **to put o.s. out:** sich Umstände machen, Mühe auf sich nehmen.
16 **to have a quiet smoko** (coll.): in Ruhe eine rauchen.
22 **to tuck s.o. up:** jdn. zudecken, ins Bett stecken.

tea-tin. Brinkman sat there, as solid as his chair. "You may be wondering who I am," he said. "I'm a neighbour, come over for dinner. I think of myself as one of the perpetually welcome." "Suit yourself," said the sister-in-law. The doctor emerged, moving rather faster than he usually did. "Please to go in there and wash the patient. I'm going to take a look at the afterbirth. The father put it out with the waste."

There Tanner had made his one oversight. It wasn't the afterbirth, it was a second daughter, smaller, but a twin. – But how come, if both of them were girls, that Mr Tanner himself still had the name of Tanner? Well, the Tanners went on to have nine more children, some of them boys, and one of those boys was Mr Tanner's father. That evening, when the doctor came in from the yard with the messy scrap, he squeezed it as though he was wringing it out to dry, and it opened its mouth and the colder air of the kitchen rushed in and she'd got her start in life. After that the Tanners always had one of those tinplate mottoes hung up on the wall – Throw Nothing Away. You could get them then at the hardware store. – And this was the point that Mr Tanner had been wanting to make all along – whereas the first daughter never got to be anything in particular, this

4 **perpetually** (adv.): ständig.
7 **afterbirth:** Nachgeburt.
9 **to make one's one oversight:** eine einzige Sache übersehen, sich ein einziges Mal versehen.
16 **messy:** schmutzig, verschmutzt.
scrap: hier: Häuflein, Bündel.
20 **tinplate:** Zinnteller.

second little girl grew up to be a lawyer with a firm in Wellington, and she did very well.

All the time Brinkman continued to sit there by the table and smoke his pipe. Two more women born into the world! It must have seemed to him that if this sort of thing went on there should be a good chance, in the end, for him to acquire one for himself. Meanwhile, they would have to serve dinner sometime.

2 **Wellington:** Hauptstadt von Neuseeland im Südwesten der Nordinsel.

Nadine Gordimer

Homage

Read my lips.

Because I don't speak. You're sitting there, and when the train lurches you seem to bend forward to hear. But I don't speak.

If I could find them I could ask for the other half of the money I was going to get when I'd done it, but they're gone. I don't know where to look. I don't think they're here, any more, they're in some other country, they move all the time and that's how they find men like me. We leave home because of governments overthrown, a conscript on the wrong side; no work, no bread or oil in the shops, and when we cross a border we're put over another border, and another. What is your final destination? We don't know; we don't know where we can stay, where we won't be sent on somewhere else, from one tent camp to another in a country where you can't get papers.

I don't ever speak.

They find us there, in one of these places – they found me and they saved me, they can do anything, they got me in here with papers and a name they gave me; I bur-

2 **homage:** Wertschätzung, Ehrerbietung.
5 **to lurch:** rucken.
13 **conscript:** Wehrpflichtiger, Einberufener.

ied my name, no one will ever dig it out of me. They told me what they wanted done and they paid me half the money right away. I ate and I had clothes to wear and I had a room in a hotel where people read the menu outside three different restaurants before deciding where to have their meal. There was free shampoo in the bathroom and the key to a private safe where liquor was kept instead of money.

They had prepared everything for me. They had followed him for months and they knew when he went where, at what time – although he was such an important man, he would go out privately with his wife, without his state bodyguards, because he liked to pretend to be an ordinary person or he wanted to be an ordinary person. They knew he didn't understand that that was impossible for him; and that made it possible for them to pay me to do what they paid me to do.

I am nobody; no country counts me in its census, the name they gave me doesn't exist: nobody did what was done. He took time off, with his wife by the arm, to a restaurant with double doors to keep out the cold, the one they went to week after week, and afterwards, although I'd been told they always went home, they turned into a cinema. I waited. I had one beer in a bar, that's all, and I came back. People coming out of the cinema didn't show they recognised him because people in this country like to let their leaders be ordinary. He took his wife, like any ordinary citizen, to that corner

5 **menu:** Speisekarte.
7 f. **liquor:** Alkohol, alkoholisches Getränk, Spirituosen.
18 **census:** Volkszählung.

where the entrance goes down to the subway trains and as he stood back to let her pass ahead of him I did it. I did it just as they paid me to, as they tested my marksmanship for, right in the back of the skull. As he fell and as I turned to run, I did it again, as they paid me to, to make sure.

She made the mistake of dropping on her knees to him before she looked up to see who had done it. All she could tell the police, the papers and the inquiry was that she saw the back of a man in dark clothing, a leather jacket, leaping up the flight of steps that leads from the side-street. This particular city is one of steep rises and dark alleys. She never saw my face. Years later now (I read in the papers) she keeps telling people how she never saw the face, she never saw the face of the one who did it, if only she had looked up seconds sooner – they would have been able to find me; the nobody who did it would have become me. She thinks all the time about the back of my head in the dark cap (it was not dark, really, it was a light green-and-brown check, an expensive cap I'd bought with the money, afterwards I threw it in the canal with a stone in it). She thinks of my neck, the bit of my neck she could have seen between the cap and the collar of the leather jacket (I couldn't throw that in the canal, I had it dyed). She thinks of the shine of the leather jacket across my shoulders under the puddle of light from a street-lamp

3 f. **marksmanship:** Treffsicherheit.
4 **skull:** Schädel.
21 **check:** Karo(muster).
27 **puddle:** Pfütze.

that stands at the top of the flight, and my legs moving so fast I disappear while she screams.

The police arrested a drug-pusher they picked up in the alley at the top of the steps. She couldn't say whether or not it was him because she had no face to remember. The same with others the police raked in from the streets and from those with criminal records and political grievances; no face. So I had nothing to fear. All the time I was being pushed out of one country into another I was afraid, afraid of having no papers, afraid of being questioned, afraid of being hungry, but now I had nothing to be afraid of. I still have nothing to fear. I don't speak.

I search the papers for whatever is written about what was done; the inquiry doesn't close, the police, the people, this whole country, keep on searching. I read all the theories; sometimes, like now, in the subway train, I make out on the back of someone's newspaper a new one. An Iranian plot, because of this country's hostility towards some government there. A South African attempt to revenge this country's sanctions against some racist government there, at the time. I could tell who did it, but not why. When they paid me the first half of the money – just like that, right away! – they didn't tell me and I didn't ask. Why should I ask; what government, on any side, anywhere, would take me in. They were the only people to offer me anything.

And then I got only half what they promised. And

3 **drug-pusher:** Pusher, Dealer, Drogen-, Rauschgifthändler.
6 **to rake s.o. in:** jdn. auflesen.
8 **grievance:** Beschwerde.

there isn't much left after five years, five years next month. I've done some sort of work, now and then, so no one would be wondering where I got the money to pay the rent for my room and so on. Worked at the racecourse, and once or twice in night-clubs. Places where they don't register you with any labour office. What was I thinking I was going to do with the money if I had got it all, as they promised? Get away, somewhere else? When I think of going to some other country, like they did, taking out at the frontier the papers and the name of nobody they gave me, showing my face –

I don't talk.

I don't take up with anybody. Not even a woman. Those places I worked, I would get offers to do things, move stolen goods, handle drugs: people seemed to smell out that somehow I'd made myself available. But I am not! I am not here, in this city. This city has never seen my face, only the back of a man leaping up the steps that led to the alley near the subway station. It's said, I know, that you return to the scene of what you did. I never go near, I never walk past that subway station. I've never been back to those steps. When she screamed after me as I disappeared, I disappeared for ever.

I couldn't believe it when I read that they were not going to bury him in a cemetery. They put him in the bit of public garden in front of the church that's near the subway station. It's an ordinary-looking place with a

5 **racecourse:** (Pferde-)Rennbahn.

few old trees dripping in the rain on gravel paths, right on a main street. There's an engraved stone and a low railing, that's all. And people come in their lunch-hour, people come while they're out shopping, people come up out of that subway, out of that cinema, and they tramp over the gravel to go and stand there, where he is. They put flowers down.

I've been there. I've seen. I don't keep away. It's a place like any other place, to me. Every time I go there, following the others over the crunch of feet on the path, I see even young people weeping, they put down their flowers and sometimes sheets of paper with what looks like lines of poems written there (I can't read this language well), and I see that the inquiry goes on, it will not end until they find the face, until the back of nobody turns about. All that will never happen. Now I do what the others do. It's the way to be safe, perfectly safe. Today I bought a cheap bunch of red roses held by an elastic band wound tight between their crushed leaves and wet thorns, and laid it there, before the engraved stone, behind the low railing, where my name is buried with him.

1 **gravel:** Kies.
2 **to engrave:** (ein)gravieren.
3 **railing:** Geländer, Umzäunung.
10 **crunch:** Knirschen.
19 **elastic band:** Gummiband.

Rose Tremain

The Beauty of the Dawn Shift

When Hector S set out on his journey to Russia, he was wearing his uniform. It was his winter uniform, made of woollen serge, because this was December in East Berlin. While packing his knapsack, Hector S had told himself that he would have to travel in his uniform, that he had no choice; he didn't possess any other really warm clothes and where he was going, it would be as cold as death.

He was a man with a narrow frame, not tall, with pale, anxious eyes. Women thought him beautiful, but found him frigid. He was twenty-eight and he'd slept with only one girl. This one girl was his sister, Ute.

Ute kept a pet swan in a lean-to hutch on the apartment estate. She'd named it Karl and fed it on sunflower seeds. Morning and evening, she'd let it out to peck the grass and it allowed her to stroke its neck. There were no lakes or rivers in Prenzlauer Berg, the

2 **dawn shift:** Frühschicht.
5 **serge:** Serge (Gewebe).
6 **knapsack:** Tornister.
13 **frigid:** frigide, gefühlskalt, frostig.
15 **lean-to:** Anbau.
hutch: Verschlag, Käfig, Stall.
18 **to peck s.th.:** an etwas picken, hacken.
19 **Prenzlauer Berg:** Bezirk in Ostberlin.

suburb of East Berlin where they lived, and when Hector informed Ute that he was leaving for Russia, she asked him to take her and Karl with him. But he told her it was impossible, that he had to go alone with almost nothing, just his bicycle and a bag of tinned food and his rifle. He told her he couldn't travel across Poland with a swan.

Ute took this badly. She clutched at Hector's arm. She was already imagining the beautiful Russian lake where Karl would remember the lost art of swimming.

"Hecti," she said, "don't leave us behind!"

Hector S disliked emotional scenes. When their mother, Elvira, had died in 1980 Hector had basked in the wonderful quiet that descended suddenly upon the apartment. He told Ute that it was different for her, that she would be able to fit in to the New Germany and that she had nothing to be afraid of. She began to cry in exactly the same way Elvira used to cry, grabbing two hunks of her hair and saying she hated being alive. Hector walked away from her. One part of him wanted to say: "When I get there, Ute, I promise I will send for you," but another part of him wanted to remain as silent as the tomb, and on this occasion it was the tomb that prevailed.

Hector's father, Erich, on the other hand, didn't try to persuade his son to take him with him; neither did he try to persuade him not to leave. All he said was: "A

8 **to clutch at s.th.:** sich an etwas klammern.
13 **to bask:** (fig.) sich sonnen.
19 **hunk:** (großes) Stück; hier: Büschel.
23 **tomb:** Grab.

frog in a well says that the sky is no bigger than the mouth of the well, but now you have to become something else, Hector, and see the whole fucking sky. In the old imperial fairy-tales, frogs turn into princes, eh?" And he slapped his knee.

Hector replied that he had no intention whatsoever of turning into a prince.

"So," said Erich, "what are you going to become?"

"I don't know," said Hector. "Don't ask me yet."

"All right," said Erich, "but remember, when you walk away from one place, you are inevitably walking towards another."

"I know that," said Hector. "That's why I'm going east."

What should Hector take with him? This question troubled him more than many others. His knapsack wasn't large. It was the bag in which he carried his lunch or his supper, depending on which shift he was working. He would make more room in it by attaching his water bottle to the outside of it. Then there were the two saddle bags on his bicycle, but this was all. He decided, eventually, to line the saddle bags with underwear and socks. Then he put in jars of dill pickles and some plastic cutlery. He tucked these in with maps of Poland and the Brandenburg Marshes. He added a compass made

4 **imperial:** kaiserlich; erhaben, glanzvoll; hier vermutl. auch: imperialistisch.
fairy-tale: Märchen.
5 **to slap one's knee:** sich auf die Knie klatschen, schlagen.
23 **pickles:** allg.: süßsauer eingelegtes Gemüse; speziell: saure Gurken.
24 **cutlery:** Besteck.
to tuck s.th. in: etwas hineinstopfen, -klemmen.

in Dresden and five boxes of matches. The knapsack he filled almost entirely with tinned meat, wrapped in a woollen sweater. There was room for a torch and two spare batteries, a notebook and a pen. He put in a solitary lemon. He packed no books, only a small photograph album, filled with pictures of Ute, including one of her naked, developed privately by a colleague of Hector's who had dreams of becoming a professional photographer. In the naked photograph, Ute was leaning on a stool with her back to the camera and her bottom was very pale in the bleached light of early morning. Her legs looked skinny and her soft blonde hair parted at the back and hung forward, revealing her narrow white shoulders.

Hector didn't tell Ute or Erich when he was going to leave, because he thought farewells were futile and also because he didn't really know. He had to set off before the lemon in his knapsack went rotten, that was all. He knew he would recognise the moment when it came – and he did. It was the morning of 9 December 1989, one month exactly after the Wall had started to come down. He was alone in the apartment. He had exchanged all the money he possessed for D-Marks at the humiliating rate of 10-1. It amounted to DM 143 and he laid it out on the kitchen table and looked at the blue and pink notes, then gathered them up, stuffed them into his wallet and put on his greatcoat and his hat. It

4 f. **solitary:** einzeln, einzig.
11 **bleached:** gebleicht, bleich.
16 **futile:** vergeblich.
24 **to humiliate:** demütigen.
27 **greatcoat:** Wintermantel.

was a fine morning, cold and clear. He walked to the window and looked out at the blocks of flats and the scuffed grass in between them where a few children played. He remembered being told: "At the time of Tsar Nicolas II in Russia, the children of the poor had no toys of any kind. They invented games with knuckle bones." And now, thought Hector, the parents of these children will save on food and light to buy their kids sophisticated toys from the West. He felt glad he had no children, nor would ever have any because his sperm count was too low. At least he wouldn't have to choose between absolute needs and infantile ones. He was a man who had always known what was important in life and what was not.

He turned away from the window and picked up his knapsack. He looked at the room he was in, the room where the family ate and played cards and watched TV, and wondered if, when he arrived at his destination, he would think about this room and feel homesick for the black plastic chairs and the painted sideboard and the wall-mounted electric fire. He knew that memory was as uncertain in its behaviour as the sea; it could wash you ashore on any old forgotten beach; it could try to drown you in remorse. But he decided, no, it wouldn't be the apartment he would miss, only certain moments

3 **scuffed:** abgewetzt, -genutzt.
10 f. **sperm count:** Anzahl der Spermien (in der Samenflüssigkeit).
12 **infantile:** infantil, kindlich; kindisch.
19 **to feel homesick for s.th.:** Heimweh nach etwas haben.
21 **wall-mounted:** an der Wand befestigt, in die Wand eingelassen.
24 **remorse:** Reue.

in it, certain moments at dawn, just after Erich had left for work at the cement works on the Landwehr Kanal, when he walked from his own room into Ute's and got into her bed.

It is best to leave now, Hector told himself. Don't dwell on Ute.

So he walked out of the apartment without looking at anything more and went down the six flights of concrete stairs to the lobby where the post boxes had been installed. These he stared at. Neighbours passed him and said, "Good morning, Hector," and still he contemplated the metal post boxes. imagining news of his future life arriving one day inside them.

He took small roads out of Prenzlauer Berg and the streets were mainly deserted. These days, East Berliners trekked into the West to see what their few D-Marks would buy. He saw what they came back with: coloured shoelaces and luminous condoms. A lot of what they chose seemed to be a bright fearful pink or a harsh lime green, and these objects reminded Hector of the day when he'd been stopped by a group of Wessies, dressed in pink and green shell suits, who had asked him the way to Alexanderplatz. "What have you

5 f. **to dwell on s.o.:** (in Gedanken) bei jdm. verweilen, sich länger mit jdm. befassen.
16 **to trek:** in Scharen ziehen.
18 **shoelace:** Schuhband.
luminous: farbig, leuchtend.
20 **harsh:** grell (Farbe).
lime green: hellgrün.
22 **shell suit:** etwa: Jogginganzug.

come to see?" he'd asked them, more out of habit than out of interest, and they had laughed and swigged expensive beer and said: "Oh, we've come to the East German closing-down sale! Many bargains. Everything must go." And it had been at this moment and not at any other that Hector S had decided to leave his country and leave Ute and cycle to Russia. He said to himself, I'm not going because I'm afraid. I'm going because these people make me feel sick.

He joined the Leninallee and pedalled towards Lichtenberg. His back ached with the heaviness of the knapsack and the awkwardness of his rifle. Elvira was buried in the Socialists' Cemetery at Lichtenberg and it now occurred to Hector to make a small detour to look one last time at his mother's grave. He thought that he would confide to her his passion for Ute and in this way try to leave it behind. In her life, Elvira had relished confidences, licking her sensual lips ... "oh so delicious, Hecti! Tell me more!"

When he reached the cemetery, he couldn't remember where Elvira's grave was. There were so many hundreds of people buried here and he hadn't visited the place in five years. He knew he could spend hours looking for Elvira and then it would get dark and he'd still only be on the outskirts of Berlin. This would be a stupid way to waste the first day of his long journey.

2 **to swig:** herunterkippen, in einem Zug austrinken.
12 **awkwardness:** Unhandlichkeit.
14 **detour:** Umweg.
16 **to confide:** anvertrauen.
17 **to relish:** genießen.

Then he found her: *Elvira S 1931–1980*. A small polished stone. Hector parked his bicycle and took off his knapsack and rifle, flexing his shoulders. He removed his hat and stood, measuring the stone in his mind. The stone looked smaller than she had been. Did the state stone-cutters cheat on everyone by a few centimetres? And if they did, was this a thing of importance? Probably not. There were so many hundreds of millions of dead under the earth, it was amazing there was any earth left on which to grow cabbages or build kindergarten schools.

Before he could form any thoughts or words on the subject of Ute, Hector was disturbed by movement quite near him. He turned and looked and saw that a young man, poorly dressed, was going from grave to grave with a trowel, brazenly digging up the bulbs planted on them and putting them into a plastic carrier bag. The youth didn't seem to have noticed Hector – a figure of authority in a winter uniform – or else he *had* noticed him and was now deliberately taunting him with his distasteful little crime.

"Hey!" called Hector. "Don't do that!"

The youth looked up. A white face, blank, without expression. No fear in the eyes.

"Who are you?" he said.

"Border Police," announced Hector.

3 **to flex:** (Muskeln) dehnen, beugen.
6 **stone-cutter:** Steinmetz.
16 **trowel:** Maurerkelle.
brazenly (adv.): dreist, schamlos.
20 **to taunt:** foppen, aufziehen, verspotten.
21 **distasteful:** geschmacklos, widerwärtig.

"*Border* Police?"

"Yes."

The youth stood up straight and laughed. "Border Police! The border is down, or didn't anyone tell you? You mean they didn't tell you?"

"Please leave," said Hector, "before I have you arrested."

The youth didn't move. He made an obscene gesture with his hand. "*You* leave!" he said. "You fuck off out of my world!"

Hector was used to insults. Insults had been part of his life for six years and now they troubled him no more than a few flakes of snow, say, or a shower of leaves blown across his path by the wind. Except that, under normal circumstances, he had his rifle with him and at this moment his rifle was a few feet away, leaning against a tree.

"You are stealing flowers from the dead," said Hector.

The youth had a high-pitched laugh, the laugh of a girl. "Ah, you think the dead planted them, do you, Border Guard? You think they stuck their bones up into the soil to make little holes for these bulbs?"

"This is a graveyard ..." began Hector.

"Is it?" said the youth. "Oh, I thought it was a communist rubbish dump. It contains the scum who made our

9 **to fuck off** (slang): sich verpissen.
13 **flake:** (Schnee-)Flocke.
20 **high-pitched:** hoch (Stimme).
24 **graveyard:** Friedhof.
26 **rubbish dump:** Müllkippe.
scum: Abschaum, Pack, Gesindel.

lives a misery and a farce for forty years. But it's changing now, right? Every fucker in here was *wrong*! And I tell you what they're going to do with this place. They're going to bring in the bulldozers and dig up these stiffs and use them to put out Russian reactor fires and then when they've vacated it, they're going to –"

Hector walked three paces to his right and picked up his rifle. The click the youth heard was the release of the safety catch. The click stopped the flow of words and the pale face looked blank once again.

"Leave," said Hector. "Leave now."

"OK, OK," said the youth and put up his hands, one of which still held the bulb bag. The putting up of hands was a gesture which Hector had been trained to ignore when necessary. He aimed the rifle at the youth's groin.

"Hey," said the youth, "don't kill me! I know you bastards. Don't kill me!"

"Go, then," said Hector. "Go."

The youth tried to walk away backwards, keeping his eyes on Hector's gun. He stumbled over a grave and fell down and the bag of bulbs dropped out of the hand with which he tried to save himself. Then he got to his feet and ran.

So there were no confidences shared with Elvira, nothing to make her lick her lips, or bring on one of her

5 **stiff** (slang): Toter, Leiche.
6 **to vacate:** räumen.
10 **safety catch:** Sicherungshebel, Entsicherung.
17 **groin:** Leistengegend.

storms of weeping. And Ute wasn't left behind, but was carried onwards in Hector's heart.

Hector was sitting now in a café in Marzahn, the last housing estate in East Berlin, built to accommodate 160,000 people in 60,000 apartments, 2.6 humans to a unit. Beyond Marzahn were the Brandenburg Marshes and the wide open sky.

Hector had come to the café because after what happened at the cemetery, he'd started to feel chilly. He sat at a plastic table with his hands round a cup of coffee and the life of the café went on as if he wasn't there. He hoped that, in Russia, people would talk to him more, in whatever language they could muster. He really didn't want these familiar small sufferings – feeling cold inside, being ignored by people in public – to go on for the rest of his life. But nor would he ever pretend to be something other than what he was. It wasn't his fault if ideologies had a finite life span, if his world was falling away like flesh from bone, a little more each day. He'd been a communist and a patriot. He wanted to stand up in this cheap Marzahn café and say: "My name is Hector S and, to me, the word 'patriot' is not a dirty one."

He sat in the café for a long time. He smoked four Karos. He went to the toilet and pissed and washed his

4 **housing estate:** Wohnsiedlung.
9 **to feel chilly:** frieren.
13 **to muster:** aufbringen, zustande bringen.
18 **finite:** begrenzt.
life span: Lebenszeit.
24 f. **Karo:** ostdeutsche Zigarettenmarke.

face and hands in warm water. He stole a wedge of paper towels and put them into his overcoat pocket. He'd been told by a colleague that one of the marvels coming to East Germany in the near future would be toilet rolls printed with crossword puzzles.

Then he went out into the early afternoon and saw that it was later than he'd imagined and that a few lights were coming on in the tower blocks. Brought up to abhor waste, Hector admired the way East Germans used electricity. Light looked normal here. Across the Wall, he'd seen it become more and more startling and chaotic. On the long night shifts, he used to stare at all the rippling and blinking neon and wonder if it could, in the end, by reason of its absolute pointlessness, create blank spots in the human brain.

Now, he was leaving all the city light behind. It would hang in the sky at his back for a while and he'd be able to turn round and see its faint glow and say, "That's Berlin." And then it wouldn't even be a glow and the flicker of his cycle lamp would be all that he had to see by.

He pedalled hard. The only weapon he would have against the cold was his own blood. He grew more and more hungry and, on any ordinary trip, he would have stopped after two hours or so and opened one of the

1 **wedge:** Bündel, Packen.
8 f. **to abhor:** verabscheuen.
11 **startling:** erschreckend, bestürzend.
13 **to ripple:** schwanken, flimmern.
14 **pointlessness:** Sinnlosigkeit.
20 **flicker:** Flackern.

tins of Spam. But he'd set a rule for this journey – one meal a day and only one – and he was determined not to break it. So he just cycled on and the moon came up and then the stars, and he began to hear herons calling and see a second moon fallen into a wide and beautiful lake. To banish thoughts about Ute and her swan, he started to whistle some old tunes he'd picked up from Elvira who liked to sing to herself while she did the ironing.

Before night, Hector stopped at a village and bought bread. By torchlight, by the side of the road, he made a meal of tinned meat, bread and pickles. He wished he'd remembered to bring a plate to eat off as well as the plastic cutlery. Certain things, he thought, we take for granted so absolutely that they become invisible to us – and a dinner plate is one such thing.

He smoked a Karo and lay back on the frosty grass and looked at the stars. The exhaustion he now felt was suddenly intense. He knew he should repack the opened food, wrapping the bread carefully in its paper to keep it fresh for tomorrow. He knew also that he should search for some shelter, a shack or barn in which to sleep. But he couldn't move. He could barely lift his arm to stub out his cigarette.

So he closed his eyes. Some voice in him said, sleep, Hector. Sleep itself was warming properties. You'll be safe and everything will be safe till morning.

4 **heron:** Reiher.
22 **shack:** Hütte, Schuppen.
24 **to stub out:** (Zigarette) ausdrücken.

Hector was woken when the cold air of the night turned to mild but steady rain. There was enough light in the sky for him to see that a black slug was hanging off his tin of meat. He knew he ought to remove the slug and return what was left of the meat to his knapsack and that his ability to survive this journey depended upon such small acts of determination, but he felt incapable of eating meat that had been sucked at by a slug.

He saw now that he'd been lying by the side of a road and that at his back was a wood. Going into the wood to piss, he noticed that a narrow path ran between the trees, more or less parallel with the road. A red and yellow sign, nailed to an oak tree, said *Fitness Path* and depicted a man in the attitude of a runner. Hector decided to follow the Fitness Path. Here, he would be protected from the rain and, for as long as the track ran roughly level with the road, he wouldn't get lost. Also, he liked the idea of coming across athletes. They were a category of people he admired, patriotic, stoical and sane. He couldn't imagine an athlete stealing bulbs from graves or doing crossword puzzles on toilet paper.

By his calculations, he had about a hundred kilometres to cycle before he reached the Polish border, and if his pace was steady, he expected to do this in three days. He hoped the beautiful forest would go on and on,

3 **slug:** Nacktschnecke.
15 **to depict:** darstellen.
20 **stoical:** stoisch, gleichmütig, unerschütterlich.
21 **sane:** vernünftig.

right to the edge of his country. He took a long drink of water. Despite his short sleep, he felt revived, almost happy. Why, he thought, was I the only one of all my friends in the Border Police to go east? He imagined his old colleagues now, trying to sleep through this wet dawn, but most of them awake in fact, listening to the traffic beginning, listening to their blood beating, and none of them knowing which to worry about more – the past or the future.

Hector met no athletes, not even any amateur ones. And, to his disappointment, the Fitness Path quite soon veered north and he was forced to rejoin the road or risk becoming lost. But by this time, the sun was starting to glimmer through the rain clouds, making the road shine, and Hector's contentment didn't really diminish. It stemmed, he decided, from an acknowledgement of his own bravery. Bravery was the word. Most people in East Germany had their eyes turned towards the West, as if they were kids in a cinema queue and the West were the last show on earth. Only he, Hector S, had the courage and the vision to ride east towards the Russian winter, towards the wilderness.

He stopped at a public wash-house to shave and shower. Keeping clean was something he intended to do. He loved showers. He habitually masturbated under the shower, as did his father since the death of Elvira, and didn't care if anyone saw him do it. But here,

12 **to veer:** sich wenden, abbiegen.
14 **to glimmer:** schimmern.
15 **contentment:** Zufriedenheit.
17 **bravery:** Tollkühnheit, Tapferkeit.

the streams of hot water only soothed the ache in his back and in his calves and he had no erection. The most significant thing that he had to deny himself on this journey was Ute. He knew that his sanity and his ability to keep to his resolve depended upon this. Only when he arrived at his destination, wherever that turned out to be, would he get out the photograph of Ute leaning on the stool and take her from behind, as often as he felt inclined. And if his yearning for her then – for the real Ute, with her soft hair and her cunt that tasted of the sea – became serious like an illness, he would send for her.

He left the wash house with bright pink skin and wearing clean underwear. He went to a village café for coffee and a sweet cake and, although it was still early in the morning, there were old people dancing here, on the wooden café floor. The band consisted of an accordionist and a double bass player and these two were also old. Hector stared round him. On they danced, partner with partner, men with women, women whose men had died or been mislaid dancing together, all smiling and proud of the way they could still move their feet. Hector now realised that he was the only young person in the café and he wondered whether he was in some old persons' club and had only been served out of

1 **to soothe:** lindern.
4 **sanity:** geistige Gesundheit.
9 **yearning:** Sehnsucht, Verlangen.
10 **cunt** (vulg.): Möse, weibliches Geschlechtsteil.
18 **double bass:** Kontrabass.
21 **mislaid:** Gemeint ist vermutl. *misled* (*to be misled doing s.th.:* sich verleiten lassen, etwas zu tun).

deference to his uniform. He closed his eyes. The music was jaunty and light. A country where old people can dance in the morning must be a good country. And Hector imagined how this music could beckon people from their beds and that instead of lying under their feather quilts waiting to die, they would examine their dancing shoes for signs of wear, comb what remained of their hair, put on a shawl or a coat and walk down to the café, humming or whistling. Yet soon this scene would be annihilated by history. Hector opened his eyes and said quite loudly to an old woman who had sat down at the next table: "This dance café will be closed."

She hesitated. Had Hector just uttered an order? You could never predict what extraordinary orders were going to come out of the mouths of uniformed men. Once, she had been stopped on her way to the butcher's and told to remove her wig.

"I beg your pardon?" she said.

"Yes," said Hector. "It will be closed. In less than a year. This place will become a discotheque. They will play Western music here, pop and rock and rap, and nobody in this village will sleep, ever again. And nor will you old people dance."

Hector had finished his coffee and cake. He didn't want

1 **deference:** Respekt, Achtung.
2 **jaunty:** flott, beschwingt.
6 **feather quilt:** Federbett.
8 **shawl:** Umschlagtuch.
9 **to hum:** summen.
10 **to annihilate:** (fig.) auslöschen.
18 **wig:** Perücke.

or expect a reply. He'd said what he wanted to say and now he would just leave. The old woman stared at him as he got up and shouldered his knapsack and his rifle. The musicians watched him and the dancing couples watched him, but nobody spoke out. When Hector emerged into the street, it was raining again, a light but steady rain.

Living in this way, off his meat and dill pickles, spending a little money on hot coffee and bread and sleeping on the good German earth, Hector S reached the Polish border.

He was perhaps forty kilometres inside Poland when he fell ill.

He fell ill from cold and exhaustion and from something else he couldn't name. The illness came over him just outside the town of G, when he found himself in a landscape of striped hills, strip-farmed plough and fescue grass. And coming towards him on the quaint ribbon of road was a funeral procession, led by a priest holding a mighty cross. And it was as if he – with his bicycle and his rifle – was the only living thing in a terrible old painting and the low sunlight was the varnish on that painting, yellow and sickly. His legs, so strong when his journey had begun, felt suddenly hollow, the

17 **strip-farmed plough:** parzelliertes Ackerland.
17 f. **fescue grass:** Schwingelgras.
18 **quaint:** eigentümlich; malerisch.
22 **varnish:** Firnis (schnell trocknendes, farbloses Öl, das als Schutzschicht auf ein Gemälde aufgetragen wird).
23 **sickly:** fahl.

weight of the knapsack and rifle on his back unbearable.

And he could hear singing. It was the priest and all the mourners wailing in Polish for the dead person, and to Hector this human music was more disagreeable, even, than one of Elvira's attacks of weeping in the apartment in Prenzlauer Berg. It made his stomach heave.

He got off his bicycle and leaned his weight over the handlebars and the saddle. He wanted to get right away from the road, so that he wouldn't have to come near the mourners or smell their fusty clothes or hear them breathing as they sang, but the striped hills on either side of the road were quite steep – too steep in fact for a man who has been stricken with sickness.

It occurred to Hector in the next second that he would have to shoot the mourners down. He would start with the priest. But he felt a little confused by numbers: how many mourners and how many bullets? And confused by distance: optimum range for this calibre of rifle was … what? He once knew it by heart, just as a man knows his own name by heart. And then, he was confused by currencies and their terminology. Was "dollar" a universal word, or was there a Polish word for "dollar" that was not "dollar" differently pronounced? Was a zloty a coin or was it a note? Was it a letterbox? How

4 **mourner:** Trauernde(r).
to wail for s.o.: um jdn. klagen, jdn. beweinen.
8 **to heave:** hochkommen.
12 **fusty:** muffig.
26 **zloty:** polnische Währungseinheit.

many zlotys in a golden cross? How many letterboxes in a striped field …?

Of course, Hector felt himself begin to fall, but a person falling may not reach the ground to his certain knowledge, but instead arrive somewhere else. Hector fell on to the grey tarmac of the ribbon road and the priest and the mourners, seeing a man in a foreign uniform lying in their pathway, came on steadfastly towards him. Hector, however, is entering a different moment of time. He is reporting for duty. It is summer, perfect summer. It is dawn in East Berlin. Hector is entering the door at the base of a watchtower and he begins to climb up the concrete steps. Above him is the perfect octagonal of the tower itself, with its eight viewing windows. And through these windows will be falling … at the very moment Hector enters the octagon … at this very moment of short duration but of long residence in the mind of Hector S … will be falling the extraordinary beauty of the dawn light, arriving from the East.

When Hector woke, it was dark. He was lying in bed in a small room, painted brown and lit by an oil lamp. The flicker and fumes from the oil lamp eddied round on the brown ceiling. He could remember nothing.

4 f. **to one's certain knowledge:** mit Gewißheit, gewiß.
6 **tarmac:** Teer, Asphalt.
8 **steadfastly** (adv.): beständig, unbeirrt.
14 **octogonal:** Achteck.
23 **fumes:** Dämpfe, Qualm.
to eddy: wirbeln.

Something cold touched his face. A dampness lay on his forehead. There was the smell of roses.

Then a voice, very near, said in broken German: “Are you waking, Sir?”

Hector didn’t recall making any reply, but the same voice decided to say next: “I am a train driver.”

Then the lamplit room and the train driver and the smell of roses are removed from Hector’s consciousness and he is submerged again in sleep, while the man who was a driver of freight trains between Poznan and Warsaw got up quietly and went to talk to his wife, Katarzyna, telling her reassuringly that the German soldier had woken up and that his fever was passing.

“Good,” said Katarzyna, “so I hope he can leave tomorrow.”

“Well,” said the train driver, “we shall see.”

“I don’t want to ‘see’,” said Katarzyna, who was old and afraid and had a long memory. “I want him out of our house tomorrow. I don’t know why I had to marry a man with such a stupidly kind heart.”

“He was lying in the road, Katarzyna.”

“I don’t care where he was lying.”

He is lying in Ute’s bed. He knows he shouldn’t be here, not yet. He’d forbidden himself to come here, but here he is all the same. Outside the apartment building, in the first light of morning, Ute’s swan, Karl, is screeching in his cage. Ute is lying on top of Hector,

5 **to recall:** sich erinnern.
9 **to be submerged:** (fig.) versunken sein.
10 **freight train:** Güterzug.
12 **reassuringly** (adv.): beruhigend, beschwichtigend.
27 **to screech:** kreischen.

kissing his eyes. He isn't inside her, but he can feel his erection begin against her flat stomach, and with his encircling arms he presses her closer to him, moving her body so that her breasts rub against his chest. He whispers to her that he wants her, that he will want her for ever, that he can't help himself, that his passion for her will have no end, and she says to him sweetly, giggling, licking his ear: "Hecti, it will end when you die ..."

The dark room returned. A nightlight on a saucer had replaced the oil lamp and Hector could just make out the shape of a small window, shuttered with louvres, beyond which it was possible to imagine an icy, moonlit sky. Hector turned his head, looking for the train driver sitting beside him, but no one was there.

He lay very still. There was a wet patch in the bed and Hector supposed that he had pissed in it in his sleep, but wasn't very disconcerted because this was a thing that had gone on happening to him long after boyhood and two doctors had told him that there was nothing to be done about it.

Then, hearing a train's mournful whistle, Hector remembered that he was in Poland. He remembered the striped fields and the procession of mourners. He sat up and looked around the room for his knapsack and rifle and, not finding them, was overcome with anguish.

3 **to encircle:** umschlingen.
7 f. **to giggle:** kichern.
12 **louvres** (pl.): Jalousie.
18 **disconcerted:** bestürzt, beunruhigt.
22 **mournful:** klagend.
26 **anguish:** Todesangst, Entsetzen.

Weeping was for the weak, for people like Elvira, not for him. But in this Polish night, Hector wept and he didn't seem able to stop, however hard he tried.

After a while, he heard someone get up in the room next door and an old woman came and stood by him, wrapped in a shawl, with her hair in a grey plait. She stared at him for a few moments, then shook his shoulder quite roughly. "German soldier," she said, "stop crying, please."

Hector S lay in the little room for another day and a night. Katarzyna swore at her husband and prayed on her Bible. The train driver changed Hector's sheets and fed him beetroot soup.

Katarzyna went through Hector's knapsack and removed the lemon and made herself a beautiful jug of lemon tea. She said to the train driver: "This is the first gift I've ever had from a German. And the last."

Then Hector and his bicycle and his knapsack were helped into a truck and driven to Poznan station and put into a freight car full of cauliflowers. "I am sorry," said the train driver, "to put you with vegetables, Sir."

After this, there was just the dark of the freight car and the sound of all the miles and miles of the Polish heartland moving under the train. Hector lay down and covered himself with his overcoat and was as still as a man

6 **plait:** Zopf.
13 **beetroot:** Rote Bete.
20 **cauliflower:** Blumenkohl.
24 f. **heartland:** Landesinnere.

can be on a bed of cauliflowers. His head and body ached and it seemed to him that this ache was right in the substance of his skull and in the marrow of his bones.

His future was going wrong. Every thought that came to him, instead of being clear and precise, was clouded and difficult. It was as though thoughts were harmful chemicals, setting off explosions in his brain. The train was taking him nearer to his destination, but he began to see, with embarrassment, that it was towards the old eternal Russia of his imagination that he was travelling and that although he'd prepared quite well for his journey, he hadn't prepared at all for his arrival. When his D-Marks ran out, where and how was he to live? For a start, he spoke only a few words of the language. He knew the Russian word for "tomorrow", but not the Russian word for "now". What kind of work could he find which allowed him to be totally silent?

Then a new thought came. The colour of its chemical felt white. It was a thought about silence and the new world, the world of the West, creeping east. Westerners were thieves of silence. They stole the quiet in a place and in the mind of a man and replaced it with longing, just as they stole the mystery from a city by lighting it orange. Darkness and quiet were leaving the world. It was only a matter of time before the dawn wouldn't be the dawn any more, but some other computer-adjusted piece of time, with colours other than its own.

Hector felt pleased with this thought, not because it

3 **skull:** Schädel.
marrow: (Knochen-)Mark.

was an optimistic one, but because it seemed rational and not blighted by confusion, and so he said to himself that perhaps he was going all this way in search of the perfect silence. He'd imagined a wilderness, a birch grove, a lake, or at least, he'd imagined cycling or walking through this kind of landscape on his way to his future in Russia. But the truth was that the future had no location. He'd never got further with his own story than the lake. Now, he understood that he might never get further – ever. In all probability, the lake was his destination.

Hector sat up and tried to eat a pickled cucumber. He had no appetite for what remained of the tinned meat. He lay down again, liking the train now, soothed a bit by the train, as if the train were Elvira and Hector a child falling asleep on her lap, wrapped in her apron.

He didn't want to show his face in Warsaw. He knew he would be stared at and he couldn't abide the thought of meeting the stare of Polish women and girls.

He dreamed the place smelled of spun sugar, that there was dry rot in the old houses, that church bells kept ringing and ringing the hours, that pigeons continuously ruffled the air. He would fall ill again in such a place.

2 **to blight:** beeinträchtigen, überschatten, zunichte machen.
4 f. **birch grove:** Birkenhain, -wäldchen.
8 **location:** Ort.
12 **cucumber:** Gurke.
16 **apron:** Schürze.
20 **spun sugar:** Zuckerwatte.
21 **dry rot:** Trockenfäule.
23 **to ruffle:** in Bewegung versetzen.

So he resorted to bribery. He offered DM 10 to the train driver and asked him to put him in another freight going east to the border with Belorus or beyond.

The train driver took the money and looked at it and shook his head. "Now from here in a freight going east, you will die of cold, Sir."

"I'm used to the cold" said Hector.

"Not this one. This is more cold."

"Please," said Hector.

So the money was paid and a second driver was found who agreed to take him in a night train carrying medical supplies to Minsk. Katarzyna's husband then performed his last act of generosity: he gave Hector the blanket he kept in his cab. "In the cold night," he said, "cover your body, German man."

Hector missed the cauliflowers. In this second freight car, piled with boxes, every surface was hard and in whatever way he lay down, Hector's bones hurt. He tried folding the blanket in three and lying on top of it. This was more comfortable and Hector was beginning to drift towards sleep when he opened his eyes and saw in the darkness the freezing cloud of his own breath lying over him like a ghost. In time, he would have breathed all the air in the box car and the ghost would be very large and attempt to make more room for itself by entering the cavities of his body and taking away his life.

1 **bribery:** Bestechung.
3 **Belorus:** Weißrussland.
12 **Minsk:** Hauptstadt von Weißrussland.
22 **to freeze:** gefrieren.
26 **cavity:** Öffnung.

The blanket smelled of oil and it was old and worn, but there was still a little warmth in it. Hector stood up and wrapped himself round and round in it and lay down again on the boxes of pharmaceuticals. He imagined he was lying on glass syringes, as clear as ice.

The night would be so long. Poland, thought Hector, is a place where the nights have subdued the days and stolen half their territory. The bit of space left to the light is so pitiful, you just have time to cycle a few kilometres, buy some hard bread, pass a church where women kneel at open-air confessionals, hear a village band wearing hats with emperor's plumes play an ancient march, and then the dusk comes down, and it's futile to look forward to morning, because morning is so far away. It wasn't so mad, so completely foolish to imagine that here, on certain days, you could go into a post office, say, to buy a stamp, and that when you came out again with the stamp in your wallet, the day had given up hope and the words "post office" had faded into the wall.

These thoughts made Hector remember the line of post boxes in the lobby of the apartment building in Prenzlauer Berg and how he'd imagined letters from Russia arriving here, letters which described an epic journey, an honourable arrival, a life built in a place where the

4 **pharmaceuticals:** Pharmaerzeugnisse.
5 **syringe:** Spritze.
7 **to subdue:** verblassen lassen; besiegen, unterwerfen.
11 **confessional:** Beichte.
12 **plume:** Feder.
13 **dusk:** Abenddämmerung.
24 **epic:** waghalsig (Reise)

structures of the old familiar world were still standing.

Now, in his freight car, wrapped in the train driver's blanket, as heavy snow starts to fall, Hector begins to compose in his mind a letter to Ute, to the sister he's desired since the day, at the age of five, when she licked his penis in the bath. It may be, he thinks, the only letter he will have time to think up and so he wants it to describe a place that will seduce Ute, a place in which she will recognise that she could be happy, a place he has made safe for her in advance:

Dear Ute,

I have arrived at the loneliest, most beautiful place in the world. Let me describe it to you. It is a great forest that has been growing silently for more time than anything else on this part of the earth. Bears inhabit it. And reindeer and wolves. Snow lies over it for seven months of the year. Sometimes, I fall into conversation with a solitary hunter and we discuss weapons and the individual characteristics of flight of certain difficult targets and how, in one's aim, one may compensate for these and so kill after all and not starve. Bears are protected and may not be shot.

And this brings me to swans. At the feet of the forest is a lake. The north side of it is frozen, but a little water still laps the snow on this southern

9 **to seduce:** verführen.
17 **reindeer:** Rentier(e).
22 **to compensate for s.th.:** etwas ersetzen, ausgleichen.

side and here I have discovered a fine family of your favourite birds. They whoop like cranes in the early morning. They're plump and sleek from the quantity of fish they find in the lake. They are as tame as Karl and will come if I call them and feed from my hand. When you join me here, this is the first thing we will do: go down to the lake and visit the swans.

I expect you're wondering where we're going to live and how we're to find shelter. "Hecti," I hear you say, "are you asking me to make love to you in the snow?" No, Ute. No, I'm not. Unless you want to do that.

I have found, at the lakeside, an old grey dacha, built of wood, with a stone chimney and a steep shingled roof. I walked into it like that girl in the fairy story and sat down in the largest of the chairs. I found a smoked ham hanging inside the chimney. I found a larder full of apples. I found folded sheets for the bed.

It's as if this dacha was designed with me in mind, with everything necessary for my survival: an axe to chop wood, a fire to cook on, even a featherbed quilt for the nights, which are as cold as nights on the moon. So now, I'm able to say to you, don't

2 **to whoop:** schreien.
crane: Kranich.
3 **plump:** rundlich, wohlgenährt.
sleek: glatt, geschmeidig.
14 **dacha:** Datscha, Wochenendhaus.
16 **shingled:** mit Schindeln gedeckt.
19 **larder:** Vorratskammer.

waste any more time, sell whatever you have to sell – Elvira's hairbrushes, Father's cache of cigarettes – and take the next train out of Berlin going east …

It was at this point in his imaginary letter that Hector was jolted forwards and almost fell off the ledge of boxes on which he was lying. The train had stopped. Hector listened. He hadn't seen the thick snow falling, but by the temperature in the car and by the absence of any sound, he was able to judge that it was the deep middle of the night. The train would still be a long way from Minsk, a long way even from the border, so he supposed that it must have stopped at a signal and that in a few minutes it would get going again.

Somehow, the immobilisation of the train made the cold inside the freight car more intense and the ghost of breath that filled the space around and above Hector became agitated and began a strange kind of wailing.

The train moved. But it was going backwards, Hector could tell by the way his body rolled. And then it stopped again. Hector raised his head off his knapsack, to hear better, to see better, but he could hear and see nothing except the ghost in the air.

What Hector couldn't know was that the train had been

2 **cache:** Etui.
6 **to jolt:** (mit einem Ruck) schleudern.
ledge: Sims, Reihe, Sockel.
15 **immobilisation:** Bewegungslosigkeit, Stillstehen.
18 **agitated:** unruhig, verstört.

re-routed into a siding because the line further east was temporarily closed by snow. What he couldn't know either was that the driver of the second freight had forgotten all about him and, once the train was safe in its siding, got down from his cab and walked away across the white fields towards a village, in search of a warm fire and a bed for the rest of the night. So Hector lay there, waiting for the train to resume its journey, while the soft snow piled up on the roof of the box car.

After an hour had passed, he tried to move himself towards the edge of the car, so that he could bang on the doors with his feet, but he found that his body was unwilling to move. It asked him to let it rest. He attempted, then, to call out. He knew that a human voice inside a freight car would probably make the kind of sound that disturbed no one's peace and altered nothing in the world, but he tried to call nevertheless. "Train driver!" he said. "Help me!" It was a whisper, not a shout. Hector believed that he was shouting, but he was only murmuring. And anyway, the driver of the second freight was a mile away. He was sitting by a fire with a schoolteacher and his wife, drinking vodka and eating poppyseed cakes.

After his efforts at calling, Hector's throat felt sore and he was afflicted suddenly by a desperate thirst. He had no memory of where his water bottle was or when he

1 **to re-route:** umlenken, -leiten.
siding: Abstellgleis.
11 **to bang:** hämmern, trommeln.
23 **poppyseed:** Mohn(samen).
25 **to be afflicted by s.th.:** von etwas befallen sein, geplagt werden.

had last seen it, but what he did remember was the solitary lemon he had put into his knapsack on the morning of his departure. And his longing, now, to suck the juice from this lemon became so great that he succeeded in extracting one hand from the blanket and with this one hand reached behind his head to try to undo the fastenings of his knapsack.

He could picture with absolute precision the colour, shape and texture of the lemon as it had been when he packed it and his mind refused to imagine it any other way.

It is difficult to say how long Hector S struggled to locate this perfect yellow fruit, but into his search for it he put every last ounce of his strength.

The snow stopped falling an hour before sunrise and the sky cleared and the dawn was bright.

Woken by the winter sunlight, the driver of the freight to Minsk remembered at this instant the German soldier he'd agreed to hide in one of his box cars in return for DM 5.

He dressed hurriedly, tugging on his overcoat and his hat, and let himself out of the schoolteacher's house.

The snow was thick on the fields. The man wasn't young. Trying to make his way through this deep snow was exhausting for him and it took him the best part of half an hour to reach the train.

He opened the door of Hector's box car and stared in. The light on the snow had blinded him and, for a mo-

9 **texture:** Oberfläche.
21 **to tug s.th. on:** etwas festzurren.

ment, he could see nothing. "Hello!" he called. "Hello! It is morning."

Hector was lying face up, one arm behind his head that rested on his knapsack. His face had the pallor of bone, but there was a smile on it, as if, in his last moments, Hector had glimpsed something of great beauty.

The train driver walked a few paces from the car and fumbled to light a cigarette.

He stood in the snow, thinking.

It didn't take him long to decide what he was going to do. He was going to leave Hector exactly where he was. He wasn't even going to touch him or cover his face. Even if the day remained fine, the cold in the box car would preserve the body and, with a bit of luck, the train would get to Minsk before nightfall.

At the depot, the freight would be unloaded by rail workers from Belorus, and so it would be they who would find the stowaway. In this way, provided he remembered to get rid of the DM 5, the driver would have shifted the burden of responsibility. The dead German, wearing some kind of military uniform, would become a Russian problem.

4 **pallor:** bleiche Farbe, Blässe.
8 **to fumble:** (herum)tasten, kramen.
16 **depot:** Bahnhof.
18 **stowaway:** blinder Passagier.

Kathy Page

It Is July, Now

I ride the bus to the airport so as to keep the expenses. It takes an hour and a half and then the plane is forty-five minutes late. Well naturally, I do not take kindly to extra work at weekends and for two weeks the Director has been plaguing me to inspect the flat and before that he rejected one I had found myself, which was with someone I know: one room only and landlady *in situ* would not be suitable – they are used to having personal space, he said. A flat is a flat, I think, four walls: if one of us has lived in it, it will do for her. I did not make the inspection, but told the Director that I had. Some of the people in our Academy, I told the Director when he suggested I have a visitor in my department, are the foremost experts in their fields; it is a joy to hear them talk. But many of the foreigners who come do not even speak their own languages correctly, let alone have a proper pedagogical method or good manners. They all say that they are very interested in us and would rather be here than at home, but it is my view

3 **to keep the expenses:** die Ausgaben in Grenzen halten.
5 **to take kindly to s.th.** (coll.): von etwas begeistert sein.
7 **to plague s.o.:** jdn drangsalieren.
9 **in situ** (Lat.): ebenda, am Ort.
16 **foremost:** (fig.) führend.

that some of them come here because there is unemployment in their own countries and they are inadequate to secure positions: so I am against it.

"Even so," he said, clicking his pen in and out, as he does, "there is nothing to be lost." So it was decided.

Just as I am convinced that she has missed the plane I turn around and the person sitting on the bench behind me, wearing a dark red coat and no hat, can only be her. The coat is far too long: it will trail in the mud; the shoes will be soaked through. And her hair is cut short about her face, so that she looks like a child, but with very shiny lipstick on: the fashion, perhaps, where she comes from, but to my mind not a good one. Fashion is an odd thing. There, where they have freedom, they follow it. Here, where there has been none, we are all individuals.

"Good afternoon," I say.

"Hello." She stands up, her gloves fall on the ground, she bends straight down to pick them up, forgetting to offer her hand.

The Director also said that I should invite her to my home. A glass of wine with cheese was the done thing, he told me.

I have a whole house, in fact, only a minute from the city centre but built in the country style. Three floors, four rooms, a garden, gables: I had it painted ice-cream pink last summer. It is large enough for my daughter

9 **to trail:** (am Boden) schleifen.
10 **to be soaked through:** völlig durchnässt, klatschnass werden, sein.
22 **the done thing:** das Übliche, das, was man tut.
26 **gable:** Giebel, Dachgaube.

Katrin and me not to get in each other's skirts. She has a job at the City Hall but they won't allocate her a flat because there is enough space here. Still, I have my own study in the attic, with waxed floors, fresh curtains, a good rug, a proper office chair and a telephone extension. The house is mine – nationalised, of course, but I have the proofs and it is just a matter of time – and even you, I thought at the Director, cannot compel me to have someone in it if I do not want. He is young, very clever. Before, he was a scholar in a garret; now, he has been given a laptop computer, whereas I am paid nothing extra for being Head of Department, though it looks good on my CV, which we all have to make these days – and eventually, when the country is sorted out, it may lead to something.

The visitor's flat is in an anonymous district on the outskirts of town, big blocks with numbers and no names and because I haven't been there before I can't give good directions. The taxi driver is Russian and loses patience so I decide it is better to walk. She has some boots, she says, but they are right at the bottom of her bag, should she get them out? I tell her no.

1 **to get into each other's skirts:** etwa: übereinander stolpern.
2 **City Hall:** Rathaus.
to allocate: zuteilen.
4 **attic:** Dachgeschoss, Mansarde.
6 **to nationalise s.th.:** etwas enteignen, in Staatseigentum übergehen lassen.
7 **proofs:** hier: (Eigentums-)Nachweise.
10 **garret:** Dachkammer.
12 **Head of Department:** Institutsleiter, -direktor.
13 **CV:** Abk. für *curriculum vitae* (Lat.): Lebenslauf.

"This isn't what I imagined," she says. "What sort of place is it?"

"It is typical," I tell her. Finally we arrive. The stairs to it smell terrible: still, I think, it will probably be all right inside.

"I have never seen so many cats," she exclaims.

"Actually, I have a cat myself," I say, as I try to let us in – the lock is stiff – "it is on penicillin at the moment," I tell her, "extremely expensive, an import. People can look after themselves. But pets are helpless, they can't manage: we must take care of them!"

Finally the door opens on a narrow corridor with a room either side and the bathroom at the end. The place is extremely hot and dusty – I go straight over to open a window, but when I get it to open I see there is an old cupboard and some rotting rugs on the balcony, and the remains of a seagull in the middle of it all. I remember also that I told the visiting lecturer on the phone that I had inspected the accommodation and that it was comfortable. I want to escape. But she walks around, trying everything, even opening cupboards and flushing the toilet. She says the television does not work.

"In any case, it would be incomprehensible," I tell her.

"Well, not the pictures," she points out.

8 **to be stiff:** schwergängig sein, klemmen.
17 **seagull:** Möwe.
18 **visiting lecturer:** Gastdozent(in).
22 **to flush the toilet:** die Toilettenspülung betätigen.
24 **incomprehensible:** unverständlich.

"The programmes are of poor quality. It wouldn't interest you. Here are your fees for the three weeks." I give her the envelope. She looks at the money, puts it back in the envelope without counting it, undoes her coat. She has on a pair of close-fitting black trousers and a soft brown jumper that clings to her shape. She stretches her arms and rolls her head around.

"What next?" she asks. It is dark by now. I take her straight out to look at the shop and the bus stop and tell her that I will meet her at Kaarmanni Olletuba at eight for supper; the Academy will pay. Just then my bus comes. Anyone will know where it is, I tell her as I get on.

She wants me to write some phrases down for her.

"Really, there is no point in language lessons," I say. I have put on my suit and a brooch; she too has changed and it is a cream knitted dress now, with flecks of grey and red in it and a roll neck. "You will learn nothing in such a short time, it is extremely complex grammatically."

"I'm not talking grammar –" she says, "I just want to be able to point at a sandwich and say please. Or, for instance, to say "Can you give me directions to" rather than just barking the name of a café at some poor woman in a bus, do you see what I mean, Piret?" She has a habit of using one's name all the time.

16 **brooch:** Brosche.
17 **cream:** cremefarben, beige.
knitted dress: Strickkleid.
fleck: Tupfen.

"You are here for just three weeks," I say. "Everyone can see that you are a stranger; they won't expect it of you."

"That's not the point." I am not used to being argued with.

"We have a great deal to do," I say, firmly. We push on and cover the necessary arrangements. I am ready to go then but she is drinking her soup like a snail.

"Well, Piret," she says, "tell me about yourself."

"Here," I tell her, "we do not have small talk. We get to know each other slowly."

"I see." She plays with her bread and looks around her as if she was trying to commit the place to memory. "Could we have more wine?" That uses up the money I saved by coming on the bus.

Life is hard, I tell her while we drink it. It cannot be legislated against as you are always trying to do in the West. You have a deal – good parents, bad parents, dead parents, a good country, a bad country or in-between. However it is, you use your talents to carve a way for yourself, you just make the best of it. Some people go under. Some people complain too much. Others are too kind ... Drink makes me talk. When we at last emerge there is a strong wind blowing from the sea; the thermometer in the square shows minus fifteen. "What is your word for snow?" she asks.

8 **snail:** Schnecke.

13 **to commit s.th. to memory:** sich etwas merken, einprägen.

17 **to legislate against s.th.:** Gesetze gegen etwas einbringen, Vorschriften gegen etwas erlassen.

20 f. **to carve a way for o.s.:** (fig.) den eigenen Weg suchen.

At home, Katrin is still up, eating milk pudding and watching the Finnish television channel, very loud, and reading magazines at the same time. The magazines are dreadful. What is your wildest dream? they ask. Do you get enough? How do you rate on the passion scale? She is not an intellectual, though she could have been, perhaps it is to spite me. She is particularly difficult these days. You resent me, she often accuses. It's not my fault there's an accommodation shortage ... At least, I tell her when she complains, you have a mother, which I did not have for very long – all I remember is her brushing my hair, and coming to me in the night. I dream of that still once in a while; it's only natural. My father of course was away in the war, then died in it. Mainly I grew up in the orphanage – it was harsh, but invaluable in teaching self-reliance.

I didn't ask to be born, Katrin is always saying. You think you've done such a lot for me, but you haven't. I want nothing from you. You've never really loved me, it's only duty ... She becomes impassioned. You think he would have stayed with you, happy ever after, if not for me, she says. Don't you? We make our meals separately now. After all, she is twenty-five. Some of what she says is true, but not all.

The visiting lecturer comes to the Academy on Mon-

15 **orphanage:** Waisenhaus.
harsh: (fig.) hart.

16 **invaluable:** von unschätzbarem Wert, wertvoll, außerordentlich wichtig.
self-reliance: Selbstvertrauen.

20 **impassioned:** leidenschaftlich.

day morning. Apparently she left the bus at the wrong stop the night before and had to walk several kilometres through the snow and there was some problem with the toilet in her flat, which flooded; also drunken men banged on the door – but this is normal, I tell her, in the district where you are. She has on jeans and a silk blouse and the boots she wears are very odd. She spends the morning photocopying and uses most of the paper for the term.

I do not normally go out with subordinates, but a visitor has ambiguous status so I accept her invitation to attend a concert. "Let me treat you," she says. "Treat?"

"To treat is to pay for, but really a matter of taking turns," she explains, "of showing you'd like to provide even if you can't. It works out the same in the end."

"Here, each of us must keep to her own economy," I say. "It is simply too stressful otherwise. It is almost rude to suggest such a thing. You will embarrass people; they will feel that they have to return the favour when they simply cannot afford it."

"I'm sorry," she says and her face turns red.

The National Symphony Orchestra puts no one to shame, though the auditorium is unexpectedly full of children. I don't know why this is, I tell her in the interval. I expect they have offered the tickets free – for so-called educational purposes – and because there are so many choices these days that they cannot fill the hall.

5 **to bang:** schlagen, hämmern.
10 **subordinate:** Untergebene(r).
11 **ambiguous:** uneindeutig, schillernd.
23 **auditorium:** Zuschauerraum.

To my mind it is far too young; I did not introduce Katrin to classical music until she was seventeen, and not to jazz, which is more sophisticated, until a year after that. This accounts for these people who clap at the wrong time: they are the parents of these children; they have been forced to come, and have never before attended such an event in their lives; they simply don't know how to behave.

"Did you enjoy the music?" she asks suddenly.

As we leave she says, "May I ask you a favour? I need to call home, and none of the boxes does international calls, or am I missing something? But the phones at the Academy would do it, I think. Do you possibly have a key? Or maybe you have the right kind of telephone yourself, at home?"

"It is urgent?"

"Very," she says. I do not feel I can reasonably refuse so we go to the Academy, which seems eerie without students and colleagues being there. It is hard to find the light switches; I give up and wait in the dark on a bench in the corridor while she uses the departmental phone. I can hear her voice but not the words; perhaps she is whispering. It rises and falls and there are long silences, exclamations, laughter once or twice. It is not business, and not very urgent either. It is twenty-five minutes before she emerges, a half smile on her lips, eyes shining. When Katrin wears that kind of face, she always avoids questions, and goes straight to her room. I am angry.

18 **eerie:** unheimlich, gespenstisch.
21 **departmental:** Instituts-.

“You have dealt with the matter?”

“Oh yes, thanks, Piret,” she says, smiling.

I cannot sleep at all that night. I keep thinking of Karel, who was Katrin’s father. We were both students. It was the last year when we grew close. In summer we were both sent to do compulsory training in medical studies, so that we could fulfil our obligations if war broke out. It was in the forest, lectures all day, anatomy and so forth, but the nights were mainly our own and they were long, warm nights. We swam in the lake together, while others drank and sang patriotic songs; we despised them. Out there, beyond the reach of their voices, the water was smooth and cool as glass and afterwards our bodies were like silk. At this point I remember thinking that so long as you knew someone else who thought like you, anything was tolerable. Across whatever horrors you could hold to that connection. When we got back he came every night to my flat. It was not deliberately that I became pregnant but I do not believe in interfering with what is meant.

“But I do not believe in being trapped if there is something that can be done to prevent it,” Karel said. He took up a post in the north before she was born and I never heard from him again; I don’t even think of him often now.

The cat climbs on to my bed. It is wheezing when it

6 **compulsory:** obligatorisch.
11 f. **to despise:** verachten.
19 **pregnant:** schwanger.
26 **to wheeze:** keuchen.

purrs, but otherwise it seems all right. I smooth down its fur and it stretches out flat with its ears back; it is very comforting. I can hear Katrin snoring at the other side of the house. She has done so since a child. To start with I tried to cure her of it by waking her, but gave up.

Next it is the Post Office. I have told her the directions, but she insists on being taken. She insists also on having her letters weighed: they cost four times what they would have. Just put the stamp on, I tell her, are they going to sit at the airport weighing each one? "Maybe that's why your last to me never arrived," she says, but the fact is I did not get around to writing it. I excuse myself from lunch. There are some cheese pies at home and I want to check the cat: the vet said that since it was a virus the medicine might strengthen him but the cure was down to his natural resistance. Katrin often says I care more about that cat than I do about her, that I never made a fuss over her, though of course that is not true. It is an instinct to be tender with children, it happens whether you will it or not. She simply does not remember. Children who have their parents take things for granted. She says that I love that cat in a way I never loved her. She says that the money I spend on the cat, added up, would get her a plane ticket anywhere in Europe. She means Paris: a Frenchman came with a

1 **to purr:** schnurren (Katze).
to smooth down: glattstreichen.
3 **to snore:** schnarchen.
15 **vet:** Kurzform von *veterinarian:* Tierarzt.

trade delegation. She has many boyfriends. However, I do not allow them to stay in the house.

"This country is supposed to be *liberated*," she tells me. "There is nowhere for us to go. You are greedy," she says, "a greedy, jealous old woman ..." Sometimes, when I get in, I have a sense that someone else has been in the house, though there is never any proof. I feel the cat knows too.

Towards the end of her last week, the visiting lecturer waits outside in the corridor for me to finish my Level One class and asks for the fourth time now to go to lunch together.

"Somewhere cheap," she says, "we'll go Dutch of course."

"But actually, I am going home today," I say. "Dutch?"

"Well I can't," she says, "it takes an hour each way on the bus – you could stretch a point."

"Is there a reason?" I say. "Is there some particular academic matter you wish to discuss?"

"No," she says – her voice very even – "there isn't. Just some food and a chat. For the sake of itself." None of my regular lecturers would suggest such a thing.

"Perhaps," I say, "I can organise it so that we go out for a drink on your last night, along with the Director, who would be interested to hear what you think about our

3 **to liberate:** befreien.
4 **greedy:** gierig.
10 f. **Level One class:** Kurs der Eingangsstufe, Anfängerkurs.
13 **to go Dutch:** getrennte Kasse machen.
18 **to stretch a point:** einmal eine Ausnahme machen.

students and their progress; I can ring him this afternoon and make arrangements."

"No," she stares at me, "I was asking you, Piret, whether you wanted lunch, with me, now."

"I have told you."

"You," she said, "take the biscuit."

"The biscuit?"

"This is a one-way street," she says. Again I query the idiom. "There is no point in language lessons," she says then, and her voice turns hard: "seeing as we are never going to communicate." She turns and walks off.

It is very upsetting. Then, when I get home I walk straight up to the cat's basket to pick him up. Katrin has fed him in the morning and the wrapper from the medicine is still on the table. But he is lying there dead, his body stiff and his fur cold. My whole skin shrinks and I run back to work. I have a meeting arranged with the Director. He tells me he is going to Stockholm at Easter, for a month, paid for by the Ministry for Education; would I please take over his administration while he is away?

I tell him that the visiting lecturer is going well. I ask him for more money for books, and whether we could set the exam later in the year – after all, I say, we can

6 **to take the biscuit** (coll.): dem Fass den Boden ausschlagen, alle(s) übertreffen.
8 **to query:** in Zweifel ziehen, in Frage stellen, beanstanden.
9 **idiom:** Redewendung.
14 **wrapper:** Verpackung.
16 **to shrink:** sich zusammenziehen.

make up the rules how we want them now. He says that he will note my ideas. But he has already closed his notepad and started putting things away in drawers while I am still talking. I stay in my chair. He stands up. So everything is fine? I try to stand up too but my legs will not do it. And I try to say in a brisk, businesslike voice – oh yes, absolutely – but I cannot do that either. I say nothing at all for a few seconds, and then the words blurt out of my mouth:

"Actually, I have bad news. My cat is dead, I am just going home to bury it." But I do not want to. I do not know how to go about it, I do not want to touch it. I have had that cat for six years. He turned up on my doorstep, very thin, and I took him in. He has slept on my bed and sometimes I used to talk to him. The vet cost more than my food for a month, just for one injection, but I did not begrudge it at all. Not at all! This is how I feel. It was of course the wrong thing to say to the Director; his brother died in a labour camp, two thirds of the way through twenty-five plus five.

He puts his hat on. "There are plenty of cats," he says. "You can get another one."

I pull myself together and think how there is a chance Katrin will get home before me, and perhaps she will

3 **notepad:** Notizblock.
6 **brisk:** frisch, lebhaft, forsch.
9 **to blurt out:** herausplatzen.
17 **I did not begrudge it at all:** es war mir überhaupt nicht leid darum.
20 f. **twenty-five plus five** (*years*): Strafmaß.

wrap it up and deal with it: she's a practical sort and it would be easier for her since she didn't love it.

I decide to have the afternoon off. I need some groceries and am walking up the main street when I see the visiting lecturer on the other side. She has her hands stuck deep in her pockets and that, I think, is because she will keep leaving her gloves on the desk by the copier. One of the brass buttons is missing from her coat. I stop walking. I want to turn and go away, but instead I just freeze, watching her peer into the shops as if she had never seen things before. And it seems to me that she looks sad. And suddenly I know what it must be like to be unable to speak or understand a word of the language, not even guess at it, to get everything half right or wrong. It must be like walking around with a shell around you which no one could get through, hard outside but very, very tender beneath.

At that moment she sees me, crosses the street, shouting "Piret! How are you!" even though it is only hours since she asked the same thing in the corridor, and even though we parted on a bad note. I do not understand, and again I find myself saying something unintended: "You?" I ask. "How are you? You have not been lonely on your visit here, I hope?" She laughs. I burst into tears. It is very embarrassing.

She takes hold of my arm. "We'll go in here," she says. I am crying so much that I can't see where she means. It turns out to be the new place, Palace Café, with a pink marble floor. It is very warm inside. All the

10 **to freeze:** erstarren.
to peer: spähen.

crockery has a broad gold rim. The coffee is strong, and they serve it with chocolate truffles on a saucer. In the middle of the ceiling hangs a huge chandelier, a strange thing made from liqueur glasses and bits of welded kitchen implements, and the chains from sink plugs: postmodernist, perhaps. I find I quite like it.

"This is a very expensive place," I say, "for tourists only."

"Let's have something else," she insists, "brandy, pastries, whatever. Look," she says, opening her purse. "This is worth nothing at home, I'll only have to put it in the airport charity box."

When everything is there on the table and the waitress has gone, she asks: "Are you going to say what the matter out there?"

"No. There is a great space," I explain to her, "where nothing can be said. It is not personal." There is silence and she bites into a pastry, filling her mouth. She dusts her fingers, swallows, looks up.

"These," she says, "are the best thing I've eaten since I came here. They remind me a bit of something I had in Greece but those had mint in them too." She smiles

1 **crockery:** Geschirr.
rim: Rand.
2 **truffle:** (Schokoladen-)Trüffel.
3 **chandelier:** Kronleuchter, Lüster.
4 **liqueur:** Likör.
to weld: (zusammen)schweißen.
5 **implement:** Gerät.
12 **charity box:** Spendenbüchse.
18 **to dust:** abwischen.
22 **mint:** Minze.

lightly, as if none of the things that have taken place between us had ever been.

"We have mint ones," I find myself saying. "At Easter." Again, it is not intended, but the feeling is of it slipping out, rather than jumping.

"Do you? Does it grow here?" She pats her lips with a serviette. I wonder how old she is. Anywhere between thirty and forty, it is hard to tell. Like me, she has no wedding ring.

"I have two types in my garden," I tell her. "It dies and then comes up again, very reliable. Of course, you can dry it for winter ..." She takes a lemon cake, I a cinnamon biscuit.

"The biscuit," I say, and we laugh. I tell her more about my garden, how I prepare the soil for carrots, and how I store them. I tell her about the different kinds of daffodil bulb. Every now and then, between mouthfuls, she asks me to clarify: you have to put those under glass I suppose? What time of year would that be? And I think: how easy these things are to say! The content, I sense, is not the point at all. Yet at any minute, I think also, she could ask me something I don't want to answer. At the same time the feeling of waiting for this to happen is almost a pleasure and I am somehow disappointed when finally the bill comes and it has not occurred. They bring our coats.

"Can we go back to your house?" she says.

6 **to pat:** be-, abtupfen.
12 f. **cinnamon:** Zimt.
16 f. **daffodil:** Narzisse.
18 **to clarify:** erläutern.

She does not at all mind burying the cat for me, though the ground is still frozen, so it has to be a shallow hole. I watch from the kitchen window as she stamps the earth flat. Afterwards we drink some wine and she goes home in a taxi. I pay for it because she has spent all her money in the café, but I don't mind.

Two days later, I see her to her plane.

"Life goes on, Piret," she says. We embrace. I watch her through the passport control. "I'll write," she calls at the last minute.

But no letter has come and it is July now. The peonies were particularly good this year, the lettuce was early. I have not replaced the cat, but I planted a new lilac close to where it is, yet not so close as to disturb it. Death is always such a shocking thing: it makes one reconsider Life. Once, here, that seemed endless; now it feels shorter all the time. I would like someone from outside to tell these things to.

11 **peony:** Pfingstrose.
13 **lilac:** Fliederstrauch.
15 f. **to reconsider:** neu überdenken.

Antonia S. Byatt

A Lamia in the Cevennes

In the mid-1980s, Bernard Lycett-Kean decided that Thatcher's Britain was uninhabitable, a land of dog eat dog, lung-corroding ozone and floating money, of which there was at once far too much and far too little. He sold his West Hampstead flat and bought a small stone house on a Cevenol hillside. He had three rooms, and a large barn, which he weatherproofed, using it as a studio in winter and a store-house in summer. He did not know how he would take to solitude, and laid in a large quantity of red wine, of which he drank a good deal at first, and afterwards much less. He discovered that the effect of the air and the light and the extremes of heat and cold were enough, indeed too much, with-

2 **lamia:** in der antiken Mythologie kinderraubender und männermordender weiblicher Dämon, halb Schlange, halb Frau.
Cevennes (pl.): Bergkette am Südostrand des französischen Zentralmassivs.
4 **uninhabitable:** unbewohnbar.
4 f. **land of dog eat dog:** (fig.) Land, in dem jeder gegen jeden kämpft; Ellbogengesellschaft.
5 **lung-corroding:** die Lungen zersetzend.
floating money: frei verfügbares Kapital, (hohe) Liquidität.
7 **West Hampstead:** Stadtteil von London.
8 **Cevenol:** zu den Cevennen gehörig, in den Cevennen.
9 **to weatherproof:** wetterfest machen.
11 **solitude:** Einsamkeit.

out alcohol. He stood on the terrace in front of his house and battled with these things, with mistral and tramontane and thunderbolts and howling clouds. The Cevennes is a place of extreme weather. There were also days of white heat, and days of yellow heat, and days of burning blue heat. He produced some paintings of heat and light, with very little else in them, and some other paintings of the small river which ran along the foot of the steep, terraced hill on which his house stood; these were dark green and dotted with the bright blue of the kingfisher and the electric blue of the dragonflies.

These paintings he packed in his van and took to London and sold for largish sums of the despised money. He went to his own Private View and found he had lost the habit of conversation. He stared and snorted. He was a big man, a burly man, his stare seemed aggressive when it was largely baffled. His old friends were annoyed. He himself found London just as rushing and

2 **mistral:** Mistral (kalter Nordwestwind in Südfrankreich).
3 **tramontane:** Tramontana (kalter Nordwind aus den Alpen, v. a. in Oberitalien).
thunderbolt: Donnerschlag.
9 **terraced:** terrassiert.
10 **dotted:** gesprenkelt.
11 **kingfisher:** Eisvogel.
11 f. **dragonfly:** Libelle.
14 **largish:** ziemlich groß, beträchtlich.
to despise: verachten.
16 **to snort:** schnauben.
17 **burly:** dick, stämmig.
18 **baffled:** verblüfft.
19 **rushing:** hektisch.

evil-smelling and unreal as he had been imagining it. He hurried back to the Cevennes. With his earnings, he built himself a swimming-pool, where once there had been a patch of baked mud and a few bushes. It is not quite right to say he built it. It was built by the Jardinerie Emeraude, two enterprising young men, who dug and lined and carried mud and monstrous stones, and built a humming power-house full of taps and pipes and a swirling cauldron of filter-sand. The pool was blue, a swimming-pool blue, lined with a glittering tile mosaic, and with a mosaic dolphin cavorting amiably in its depths, a dark blue dolphin with a pale blue eye. It was not a boring rectangular pool, but an irregular oval triangle, hugging the contour of the terrace on which it lay. It had a white stone rim, moulded to the hand, delightful to touch when it was hot in the sun. The two young men were surprised that Bernard

4 **baked:** verhärtet, ausgetrocknet.
6 **jardinerie:** *le jardinage* (Fr.): Gärtnerei, Gartenbaubetrieb.
Emeraude: sprechender Name (*une émeraude* [Fr.]: Smaragd).
8 **to hum:** summen.
power-house: Kraftwerk.
9 **to swirl:** wirbeln.
cauldron: großer Kessel.
10 f. **to glitter:** glitzern.
11 **tile:** Kachel, Fliese.
dolphin: Delphin.
to cavort: Kapriolen machen, herumtollen.
12 **amiably** (adv.): freundlich, liebenswert, gutgelaunt.
13 **rectangular:** rechteckig.
14 **triangle:** Dreieck.
to hug s.th.: sich dicht an etwas halten.
15 **rim:** Rand.
to mould: anpassen, formen.

wanted it blue. Blue was a little *moche*, they thought. People now were making pools steel-grey or emerald-green, or even dark wine-red. But Bernard's mind was full of the blue dots now visible across the southern mountains when you travelled from Paris to Montpellier by air. It was a recalcitrant blue, a blue that asked to be painted by David Hockney and only by David Hockney. He felt something else could and must be done with that blue. It was a blue he needed to know and fight. His painting was combative painting. That blue, that amiable, non-natural aquamarine was different in the uncompromising mountains from what it was in Hollywood. There were no naked male backsides by his pool, no umbrellas, no tennis-courts. The river-water was sombre and weedy, full of little shoals of needle-fishes and their shadows, of curling water-snakes and the triangular divisions of flow around pebbles and boulders. This mild blue, here, was to be seen in *that* terrain.

1 **moche** (Fr.): blöd, mies.
2 f. **emerald-green:** smaragdgrün.
5 f. **Montpellier:** Stadt an der französischen Mittelmeerküste.
6 **recalcitrant:** widerspenstig.
7 **Hockney:** David H. (geb. 1937), britischer Pop-Art-Künstler.
10 **combative:** streitsüchtig, kampfbereit; hier: aggressiv, herausfordernd.
12 **uncompromising:** kompromisslos.
15 **sombre:** dunkel, düster, trübe.
weedy: voll Unkraut, Pflanzen.
shoal: (Fisch-)Schwarm.
16 **needle-fish:** Nadel-, Eingeweidefisch.
17 f. **pebble:** Kiesel.
18 **boulder:** Felsbrocken

He swam more and more, trying to understand the blue, which was different when it was under the nose, ahead of the eyes, over and around the sweeping hands and the flickering toes and the groin and the armpits and the hairs of his chest, which held bubbles of air for a time. His shadow in the blue moved over a pale egg-shell mosaic, a darker blue, with huge paddle-shaped hands. The light changed, and with it, everything. The best days were under racing cloud, when the aquamarine took on a cool grey tone, which was then chased back, or rolled away, by the flickering gold-in-blue of yellow light in liquid. In front of his prow or chin in the brightest lights moved a mesh of hexagonal threads, flashing rainbow colours, flashing liquid silver-gilt, with a hint of molten glass; on such days lines of liquid fire, rosy and yellow and clear, ran across the dolphin, who lent them a thread of intense blue. But the surface could be a reflective plane, with the trees hanging in it, with two white diagonals where the aluminium steps entered. The shadows of the sides were a deeper blue but not a deep blue, a blue not reflective and yet lying flatly *under* reflections. The pool was deep, for the Emeraude young men envisaged much diving. The

4 **to flicker:** sich schnell bewegen.
groin: Leiste(nbeuge).
12 **prow:** Bug.
13 **mesh:** Netz.
hexagonal: sechseckig.
14 **silver-gilt:** vergoldetes Silber.
15 **molten:** geschmolzen.
18 **reflective:** reflektierend, spiegelnd.
23 **to envisage:** im Voraus annehmen, voraussehen.

wind changed the surface, frilled and furred it, flecked it with diamond drops, shirred it and made a witless patchwork of its plane. His own motion changed the surface – the longer he swam, the faster he swam, the more the glassy hills and valleys chopped and changed and ran back on each other.

Swimming was *volupté* – he used the French word, because of Matisse. *Luxe, calme et volupté.* Swimming was a strenuous battle with immense problems, of geometry, of chemistry, of apprehension, of style, of other colours. He put pots of petunias and geraniums near the pool. The bright hot pinks and purples were dangerous. They did something to that blue.

The stone was easy. Almost too blandly easy. He could paint chalky white and creamy sand and cool grey and paradoxical hot grey; he could understand the shadows

1 **to frill:** bauschen.
to fur: aufrauhen.
to fleck: sprenkeln.
2 **to shirr:** in Falten legen, kräuseln.
witless: unsinnig.
5 **to chop and change:** sich andauernd ändern.
7 **la volupté** (Fr.): Lust, Wollust.
8 **Matisse:** Henri M. (1869-1954), französischer Maler; schuf 1904 ein Gemälde mit dem Titel »Luxe, calme et volupté«.
le luxe (Fr.): Luxus.
le calme (Fr.): Ruhe, Stille.
9 **strenuous:** anstrengend.
11 **petunia:** Petunie (Balkonpflanze).
12 **purple:** Purpurrot.
14 **blandly** (adv.): sanft, schmeichelnd.
15 **chalky:** kalk-, kreide-.
creamy: beige, cremefarben.

in the high rough wall of monstrous cobble-stones that bounded his land.

The problem was the sky. Swimming in one direction, he was headed towards a great rounded green mountain, thick with the bright yellow-green of dense chestnut-trees, making a slightly innocent, simple arc against the sky. Whereas the other way, he swam towards crags, towards a bowl of bald crags, with a few pines and lines of dark shale. And against the green hump the blue sky was one blue, and against the bald stone another, even when for a few brief hours it was uniformly blue overhead, that rich blue, that cobalt, deep washed blue of the South, which fought all the blues of the pool, all the green-tinged, duck-egg tinged blues of the shifting water. But the sky has also its greenish days, and its powdery-hazed days, and its theatrical louring days, and none of these blues and whites and golds and ultramarines and faded washes harmonised in any way with the pool blues, though they all went through their changes

1 **cobble-stone:** Naturstein.
2 **to bound:** begrenzen.
5 f. **chestnut-tree:** Kastanienbaum.
6 **arc:** (Tor-)Bogen.
7 **crag:** Klippe.
8 **pine:** Pinie.
9 **shale:** Schiefer.
hump: Höcker, kleiner Hügel.
14 **green-tinged:** grün getönt, mit leicht grüner Färbung.
15 f. **powdery-hazed:** etwa: mit pudrigem Dunst erfüllt.
16 **to lour:** sich (bedrohlich) verfinstern (Himmel); sich zusammenziehen (Wolken).
18 **wash:** (leicht aufgetragene) Farbe.

and splendours in the same world, in which he and his shadow swam, in which he and his shadow stood in the sun and struggled to record them.

He muttered to himself. Why bother. Why does this *matter* so much. *What difference does it make to anything if I solve this blue* and just start again. I could just sit down and drink wine. I could go and be useful in a cholera-camp in Colombia or Ethiopia. *Why bother to render the transparency in solid paint or air on a bit of board?* I could *just stop.*

He could not.

He tried oil paint and acrylic, water-colour and gouache, large designs and small plain planes and complicated juxtaposed planes. He tried trapping light on thick impasto and tried also glazing his surfaces flat and glossy, like seventeenth-century Dutch or Spanish paintings of silk. One of these almost pleased him, done at night, with the lights under the water and the dark round of the stone, on an oval bit of board. But then he thought it was sentimental. He tried veils of

1 **splendour:** Glanz, Herrlichkeit, Pracht.
4 **to mutter:** murmeln.
9 **transparency:** Durchsichtigkeit.
12 **acrylic:** Acryl(farbe).
12 f. **gouache:** dick aufgetragene Wasserfarbe in Verbindung mit Bindemittel und Deckweiß; Bild in der Technik der Gouache.
14 **to juxtapose:** nebeneinanderstellen.
15 **impasto:** dicker Farbauftrag auf einem Gemälde.
to glaze: lasieren.
16 **glossy:** glänzend, glatt.
20 **veil:** Schleier.

watery blues on white in water-colour, he tried Matisse-like patches of blue and petunia – pool blue, sky blue, petunia – he tried Bonnard's mixtures of pastel and gouache.

His brain hurt, and his eyes stared, and he felt whipped by winds and dried by suns.

He was happy, in one of the ways human beings have found in which to be happy.

One day he got up as usual and as usual flung himself naked into the water to watch the dawn in the sky and the blue come out of the black and grey in the water. There was a hissing in his ears, and a stench in his nostrils, perhaps a sulphurous stench, he was not sure; his eyes were sharp but his profession, with spirits and turpentine, had dulled his nostrils. As he moved through the sluggish surface he stirred up bubbles, which broke, foamed, frothed and crusted. He began to leave a trail of white, which reminded him of polluted rivers, of the waste-pipes of tanneries, of deserted mines. He came

3 **Bonnard:** Pierre B. (1867-1947), französischer Maler.
pastel: Pastellfarbe.
9 **to fling o.s.:** sich stürzen.
12 **hissing:** Zischen.
stench: Gestank.
12 f. **nostrils** (pl.): Nase (*nostril:* Nasenloch).
13 **sulphurous:** schweflig, Schwefel-.
14 f. **turpentine:** Terpentin.
16 **sluggish:** träge.
17 **to froth:** gischten (auf)schäumen, -sprühen.
trail: Spur.
19 **waste-pipe:** Abflussrohr.
tannery: Gerberei.

out rapidly and showered. He sent a fax to the Jardinerie Emeraude. What was Paradise is become the Infernal Pit. Where once I smelled lavender and salt, now I have a mephitic stench. What have you done to my water? Undo it, undo it. I cannot co-exist with these exhalations. His French was more florid than his English. I am polluted, my work is polluted, *I cannot go on.* How could the two young men be brought to recognise the extent of the insult? He paced the terrace like an angry panther. The sickly smell crept like marsh-gas over the flower-pots, through the lavender-bushes. An emerald-green van drew up, with a painted swimming-pool and a painted palm-tree. Every time he saw the van, he was pleased and irritated that this commercial emerald-and-blue had found an exact balance for the difficult aquamarine without admitting any difficulty.

The young men ran along the edge of the pool, peering in, their muscular legs brown under their shorts, their plimsolls padding. The sun came up over the green hill and showed the plague-stricken water-skin, ashy and

2f. **Infernal Pit:** Höllenpfuhl.
3 **lavender:** Lavendel.
4 **mephitic:** mefitisch, stinkend, verpestend.
6 **exhalation:** Ausdünstung.
florid: blumig.
10 **sickly:** übel.
11 **marsh-gas:** Sumpfgas (bei Fäulnis in Sümpfen entstehendes Gas).
14 **irritated:** gereizt, ärgerlich.
18f. **to peer in:** hineinspähen.
20 **plimsolls:** Turnschuhe.
to pad: patschen.
21 **plague-stricken:** verpestet.

suppurating. It is all OK, said the young man, this is a product we put in to fight algae, not because you *have* algae, M. Bernard, but in case algae might appear, as a precaution. It will all be exhaled in a week or two, the mousse will go, the water will clear.

"Empty the pool," said Bernard. "*Now.* Empty it now. I will not co-exist for two weeks with this vapour. Give me back my clean salty water. *This water is my life-work.* Empty it *now.*"

"It will take days to fill," said one young man, with a French acceptance of Bernard's desperation. "Also there is the question of the allocation of water, of how much you are permitted to take."

"We could fetch it up from the river," said the other. In French this is literally, we could draw it *in* the river, *puiser dans le ruisseau*, like fishing. "It will be cold, ice-cold from the source, up in the mountain," said the Emeraude young men.

"Do it," said Bernard. "Fill it from the river. I am an Englishman, I swim in the North Sea, I like cold water. Do it. *Now.*"

The young men ran up and down. They turned huge taps in the grey plastic pipes that debouched in the side of the mountain. The swimming-pool soughed and

1 **suppurating:** eiternd, eitrig.
4 **to exhale:** ausdünsten.
5 **la mousse** (Fr.): Schaum.
7 **vapour:** Dampf, Dunst.
12 **allocation:** Zuteilung, Rationierung.
16 **puiser dans le ruisseau** (Fr.): aus dem Bach schöpfen.
23 **to debouch:** einmünden.
24 **to sough:** pfeifen, sausen.

sighed and began still sighing to sink, whilst down below, on the hillside, a frothing flood spread and laughed and pranced and curled and divided and swept into the river. Bernard stalked behind the young men, admonishing them. "Look at the froth. We are polluting the river."
"It is only two litres. It is perfectly safe. Everyone has it in his pool, M. Bernard. It is tried and tested, it is a product for *purifying water.*" It is only you, his pleasant voice implied, who is pigheaded enough to insist on voiding it.
The pool became a pit. The mosaic sparkled a little in the sun, but it was a sad sight. It was a deep blue pit of an entirely unproblematic dull texture. Almost like a bathroom floor. The dolphin lost his movement and his fire, and his curvetting ripples, and became a stolid fish in two dimensions. Bernard peered in from the deep end and from the shallow end, and looked over the terrace wall at the hillside where froth was expiring on nettles and brambles. It took almost all day to empty

3 **to prance:** sich aufbäumen.
4 **to stalk:** stolzieren.
to admonish: ermahnen.
5 **froth:** Schaum.
8 **to purify:** reinigen.
9 **pigheaded:** störrisch, verbohrt.
10 **to void:** leeren.
11 **to sparkle:** glitzern, funkeln.
13 **texture:** Oberfläche.
15 **to curvet:** Luftsprünge machen.
ripple: Kräuseln, Kräuselung.
stolid: gleichmütig, stur.
18 **to expire:** hier: zerplatzen, sich auflösen.
19 **nettle:** Brennnessel.
bramble: Dornen , Brombeerstrauch.

and began to make sounds like a gigantic version of the bath-plug terrors of Bernard's infant dreams.

The two young men appeared carrying an immense boa-constrictor of heavy black plastic pipe, and an implement that looked like a torpedo, or a diver's oxygen pack. The mountainside was steep, and the river ran green and chuckling at its foot. Bernard stood and watched. The coil of pipe was uncoiled, the electricity was connected in his humming pumphouse, and a strange sound began, a regular boum-boum, like the beat of a giant heart, echoing off the green mountain. Water began to gush from the mouth of the pipe into the sad dry depths of his pool-pit. Where it trickled upwards, the mosaic took on a little life again, like crystals glinting.

"It will take all night to fill," said the young men. "But do not be afraid, even if the pool overflows, it will not come in your house, the slope is too steep, it will run away back to the river. And tomorrow we will come and regulate it and filter it and you may swim. But it will be very cold."

"*Tant pis*," said Bernard.

4 **boa-constrictor:** Riesenschlange.
4 f. **implement:** Werkzeug, Gerät.
5 f. **oxygen pack:** Sauerstoffflasche, -gerät.
7 **to chuckle:** glucksen, gluckern.
8 **coil:** Rolle.
11 **giant:** riesig.
12 **to gush:** hervor-, herausspritzen, -strömen.
13 **to trickle:** tröpfeln, rieseln.
15 **to glint:** schimmern.
22 **tant pis:** (Fr.): schade!, macht nichts!

All night the black tube on the hillside wailed like a monstrous bullfrog, boum-boum, boum-boum. All night the water rose, silent and powerful. Bernard could not sleep; he paced his terrace and watched the silver line creep up the sides of the pit, watched the greenish water sway. Finally he slept, and in the morning his world was awash with river-water, and the heartbeat machine was still howling on the river-bank, boum-boum, boum-boum. He watched a small fish skid and slide across his terrace, flow over the edge and slip in a stream of water down the hillside and back into the river. Everything smelled wet and lively, with no hint of sulphur and no clear smell of purified water. His friend Raymond Potter telephoned from London to say he might come on a visit; Bernard, who could not cope with visitors, was non-committal, and tried to describe his delicious flood as a minor disaster.

"You don't want river-water," said Raymond Potter. "What about liver-flukes and things, and bilharzia?"

1 **to wail:** wehklagen, heulen, jammern.
2 **bullfrog:** Ochsenfrosch.
6 **to sway:** hin und her schwanken, wogen.
9 **to skid:** schlittern.
13 **sulphur:** Schwefel.
15 f. **to cope with s.o.:** mit jdm. umgehen, klar-, zurechtkommen, fertigwerden.
16 **non-committal:** unverbindlich.
19 **liver-flukes:** Leberegel (Saugwürmer, die sich in den Gallenwegen und der Leber von Wild- und Haustieren, aber auch Menschen einnisten).
bilharzia: **1.** Bilharzie, Schistosome, Pärchenegel (Saugwurm, der in den Blutgefäßen schmarotzt); **2.** Bilharziose, Schistosomasis (Wurmerkrankung).

"They don't have bilharzia in the Cevennes," said Bernard.

The Emeraude young men came and turned off the machine, which groaned, made a sipping sound and relapsed into silence. The water in the pool had a grassy depth it hadn't had. It was a lovely colour, a natural colour, a colour that harmonised with the hills, and it was not the problem Bernard was preoccupied with. It would clear, the young men assured him, once the filtration was working again.

Bernard went swimming in the green water. His body slipped into its usual movements. He looked down for his shadow and thought he saw out of the corner of his eye a swirling movement in the depths, a shadowy coiling. It would be strange, he said to himself, if there were a big snake down there, moving around. The dolphin was blue in green gloom. Bernard spread his arms and legs and floated. He heard a rippling sound of movement, turned his head, and found he was swimming alongside a yellow-green frog, a frog with a salmon patch on its cheek and another on its butt, the

4 **to groan:** ächzen, stöhnen.
to sip: schlürfen.
4 f. **to relapse into s.th.:** in etwas verfallen.
8 **to be preoccupied with s.th.:** (in Gedanken) mit etwas beschäftigt, befasst sein.
14 f. **coiling:** Sich-Ringeln, Sich-Zusammenrollen (Schlange).
17 **gloom:** Dunkel.
18 **to ripple:** plätschern.
20 **salmon:** lachsfarben.
21 **butt:** Steiß.

colour of the roes of scallops. It made vigorous thrusts with its hind legs, and vanished into the skimmer, from the mouth of which it peered out at Bernard. The underside of its throat beat, beat, cream-coloured. When it emerged, Bernard cupped his hands under its cool wet body and lifted it over the edge: it clung to his fingers with its own tiny fingers, and then went away, in long hops. Bernard went on swimming. There was still a kind of movement in the depths that was not his own.

This persisted for some days, although the young men set the filter in motion, tipped in sacks of white salt, and did indeed restore the aquamarine transparency, as promised. Now and then he saw a shadow that was not his, now and then something moved behind him; he felt the water swirl and tug. This did not alarm him, because he both believed and disbelieved his senses. He liked to imagine a snake. Bernard liked snakes. He liked the darting river-snakes, and the long silver-brown grass-snakes who travelled through the grasses beside the river.

Sometimes he swam at night, and it was at night that he first definitely saw the snake, only for a few moments,

1 **roes:** eigtl.: Rogen; hier: (ausgestoßene) (Muschel-)Eier.
scallop: (Kamm-)Muschel.
vigorous: stark, heftig.
thrust: Stoß.
2 **skimmer:** hier: Abflusssieb.
8 **hop:** Sprung, Hüpfer, Satz.
10 **to persist:** anhalten, -dauern.
15 **to tug:** ziehen, zerren.
18 **to dart:** sausen, schnellen.

after he had switched on the underwater lights, which made the water look like turquoise milk. And there under the milk was something very large, something coiled in two intertwined figures of eight and like no snake he had ever seen, a velvety-black, it seemed, with long bars of crimson and peacock-eyed spots, gold, green, blue, mixed with silver moonshapes, all of which appeared to dim and brighten and breathe under the deep water. Bernard did not try to touch; he sat down cautiously and stared. He could see neither head nor tail; the form appeared to be a continuous coil like a Mobius strip. And the colours changed as he watched them; the gold and silver lit up and went out, like lamps, the eyes expanded and contracted, the bars and stripes flamed with electric vermilion and crimson and then changed to purple, to blue, to green, moving through the rainbow. He tried professionally to commit the forms and the colours to memory. He looked up for a moment at the night sky. The Plough hung very low, and the stars glittered white-gold in Orion's belt on

2 **turquoise:** türkisfarben.
4 **to intertwine:** sich (ineinander) verschlingen.
5 **velvety-black:** samtschwarz.
6 **crimson:** leuchtend rot.
peacock-eyed: Pfauenaugen-.
12 **Mobius strip:** *Möbius strip:* Möbiussches Band; von dem deutschen Mathematiker August Ferdinand Möbius (1790-1868) zur Darstellung einer einseitigen Fläche entwickelte, in sich gedrehte Papierschleife.
15 **vermilion:** Zinnoberrot.
17 f. **to commit s.th. to memory:** sich etwas merken, einprägen.
19 **the Plough:** der Große Wagen (Sternzeichen).
20 **Orion:** Sternbild.

thick midnight velvet. When he looked back, there was the pearly water, vacant.

Many men might have run roaring in terror; the courageous might have prodded with a pool-net, the extravagant might have reached for a shot-gun. What Bernard saw was a solution to his professional problem, at least a nocturnal solution. Between the night sky and the breathing, dissolving eyes and moons in the depths, the colour of the water was solved, dissolved, it became a medium to contain a darkness spangled with living colours. He went in and took notes in water-colour and gouache. He went out and stared and the pool was empty.

For several days he neither saw nor felt the snake. He tried to remember it, and to trace its markings into his pool-paintings, which became very tentative and watery. He swam even more than usual, invoking the creature from time to time. "Come back," he said to the pleasant blue depths, to the twisting coiling lines of rainbow light, "Come back, I need you."

And then, one day, when a thunderstorm was gathering behind the crest of the mountains, when the sky loured

3 f. **courageous:** mutig.
4 **to prod:** stochern.
4 f. **extravagant:** zur Übertreibung neigend.
7 **nocturnal:** nächtlich.
10 **spangled:** übersät.
15 **marking:** Spur.
16 **tentative:** vorläufig, zaghaft.
17 **to invoke:** anrufen, -flehen.
22 **crest:** Gipfel, Grat.

and the pool was unreflective, he felt the alien tug of the other current again, and looked round quick, quick, to catch it. And there was a head, urging itself sinuously through the water beside his own, and there below his body coiled the miraculous black velvet rope or tube, with its shimmering moons and stars, its peacock eyes, its crimson bands.

The head was a snake-head, diamond-shaped, half the size of his own head, swarthy and scaled, with a strange little crown of pale lights hanging above it like its own rainbow. He turned cautiously to look at it and saw that it had large eyes with fringed eyelashes, human eyes, very lustrous, very liquid, very black. He opened his mouth, swallowed water by accident, coughed. The creature watched him, and then opened its mouth, in turn, which was full of small, even, pearly human teeth. Between these protruded a flickering forked tongue, entirely serpentine. Bernard felt a prick of recognition. The creature sighed. It spoke. It spoke in Cevenol French, very sibilant, but comprehensible.

1 **unreflective:** glanzlos.
tug: Zerren, Sog.
3 f. **sinuously** (adv.): sich schlängelnd, geschmeidig.
9 **swarthy:** dunkel(häutig).
scaled: geschuppt.
12 **fringed:** fransig.
eyelashes: Wimpern.
13 **lustrous:** glänzend, strahlend.
liquid: feucht, glänzend (Augen)
17 **to protrude:** hervordringen, heraustreten.
18 **serpentine:** schlangenhaft (*serpent:* Schlange).
prick: Stich.
20 **sibilant:** zischend.

"I am so unhappy," it said.

"I am sorry," said Bernard stupidly, treading water. He felt the black coils slide against his naked legs, a tail-tip across his private parts.

"You are a very beautiful man," said the snake in a languishing voice.

"You are a very beautiful snake," replied Bernard courteously, watching the absurd eyelashes dip and lift.

"I am not entirely a snake. I am an enchanted spirit, a Lamia. If you will kiss my mouth, I will become a most beautiful woman, and if you will marry me, I will be eternally faithful and gain an immortal soul. I will also bring you power, and riches, and knowledge you never dreamed of. But you must have faith in me."

Bernard turned over on his side, and floated, disentangling his brown legs from the twining coloured coils. The snake sighed.

"You do not believe me. You find my present form too loathsome to touch. I love you. I have watched you for months and I love and worship your every movement, your powerful body, your formidable brow, the movements of your hands when you paint. Never in all my thousands of years have I seen so perfect a male being. I will do *anything* for you –"

5 f. **languishing:** sehnsuchtsvoll, schmachtend.
7 f. **courteously** (adv.): höflich, galant, zuvorkommend.
9 **enchanted:** verzaubert.
12 **immortal:** unsterblich.
15 f. **to disentangle:** entwirren.
16 **to twine:** (um)winden, -schlingen.
19 **loathsome:** hässlich, abstoßend.
21 **formidable:** gewaltig, beeindruckend.

"Anything?"

"Oh, *anything*. Ask. Do not reject me."

"What I want," said Bernard, swimming towards the craggy end of the pool, with the snake stretched out behind him, "what I want, is to be able to paint your portrait, *as you are*, for certain reasons of my own, and because I find you very beautiful – if you would consent to remain here for a little time, as a snake – with all these amazing colours and lights – if I could paint you *in my pool* – just for a little time –"

"And then you will kiss me, and we will be married, and I shall have an immortal soul?"

"Nobody nowadays believes in immortal souls," said Bernard.

"It does not matter if you believe in them or not," said the snake. "You have one and it will be horribly tormented if you break your pact with me."

Bernard did not point out that he had not made a pact, not having answered her request yes or no. He wanted quite desperately that she should remain in his pool, in her present form, until he had solved the colours, and was almost prepared for a Faustian damnation.

There followed a few weeks of hectic activity. The Lamia lingered agreeably in the pool, disposing herself wherever she was asked, under or on the water, in fig-

4 **craggy:** schroff, steil.
16 f. **to torment:** quälen.
22 **Faustian damnation:** Anspielung auf *Fausts Verdammnis* (*La damnation de Faust*, 1846), dramatische Legende des französischen Komponisten Hector Berlioz (1803-69) nach Goethes *Faust*.

ures of three or six or eight or O, in spirals and tight coils. Bernard painted and swam and painted and swam. He swam less since he found the Lamia's wreathing flirtatiousness oppressive, though occasionally to encourage her, he stroked her sleek sides, or wound her tail round his arm or his arm round her tail. He never painted her head, which he found hideous and repulsive. Bernard liked snakes but he did not like women. The Lamia with female intuition began to sense his lack of enthusiasm for this aspect of her. "My teeth," she told him, "will be lovely in rosy lips, my eyes will be melting and mysterious in a human face. Kiss me, Bernard, and you will see."

"Not yet, not yet," said Bernard.

"I will not wait for ever," said the Lamia.

Bernard remembered where he had, so to speak, seen her before. He looked her up one evening in Keats, and there she was, teeth, eyelashes, frecklings, streaks and bars, sapphires, greens, amethyst and rubious-argent.

4 **wreathing:** sich windend.
flirtatiousness: Koketterie.
oppressive: bedrückend, kaum auszuhalten.
5 **sleek:** glatt, geschmeidig.
7 **hideous:** grässlich.
8 **repulsive:** abstoßend.
17 **Keats:** John K. (1795-1821), englischer Dichter der Romantik; verfasste ein Gedicht mit dem Titel »Lamia«.
18 **frecklings:** sommersprossenähnliche Flecken, Zeichnung.
19 **sapphire:** Saphir.
amethyst: hellviolett.
rubious-argent (poet.): rubinrot-silberweiß.

He had always found the teeth and eyelashes repulsive and had supposed Keats was as usual piling excess on excess. Now he decided Keats must have seen one himself, or read someone who had, and felt the same mixture of aesthetic frenzy and repulsion. Mary Douglas, the anthropologist, says that *mixed* things, neither flesh nor fowl, so to speak, always excite repulsion and prohibition. The poor Lamia was a mess, as far as her head went. Her beseeching eyes were horrible. He looked up from his reading and saw her snake-face peering sadly in at the window, her halo shimmering, her teeth shining like pearls. He saw to his locks: he was not about to be accidentally kissed in his sleep. They were each other's prisoners, he and she. He would paint his painting and think how to escape.

The painting was getting somewhere. The snake-colours were a fourth term in the equation pool ⟩ sky ⟩ mountains ⟩ trees ⟩ paint. Their movement in the aquamarines linked and divided delectably, firing the neurones in Bernard's brain to greater and greater activity, and thus causing the Lamia to become sulkier and eventually duller and less brilliant.

"I am so *sad*, Bernard. I want to be a woman."

5 **frenzy:** Leidenschaft, Erregung.
repulsion: Ekel, Abscheu.
6 **anthropologist:** Anthropologe, Anthropologin.
6 f. **neither flesh nor fowl:** nicht Fisch und nicht Fleisch.
9 **beseeching:** flehend, bittend.
11 **halo:** Nimbus.
19 **delectably** (adv.): köstlich, reizend.
21 **sulky:** schmollend.

“You’ve had thousands of years already. Give me a few more days.”

“You see how kind I am, when I am in pain.”

What would have happened if Raymond Potter had not kept his word will never be known. Bernard had quite forgotten the liver-fluke conversation and Raymond’s promised, or threatened visit. But one day he heard wheels on his track, and saw Potter’s dark red BMW creeping up its slope.

“Hide,” he said to the Lamia. “Keep still. It’s a dreadful Englishman of the fee-fi-fo-fum sort; he has a shouting voice, he *makes jokes*, he smokes cigars, he’s bad news, *hide*.”

The Lamia slipped under water in a flurry of bubbles like the Milky Way.

Raymond Potter came out of the car smiling and carried in a leg of wild boar and the ingredients of a ratatouille, a crate of red wine, and several bottles of *eau de vie Poire William*.

“Brought my own provisions. Show me the stove.”

He cooked. They ate on the terrace, in the evening. Bernard did not switch on the lights in the pool and did

11 **fee-fi-fo-fum:** legendärer Schlachtruf der Engländer (nach Z. 1 eines Knittelverses im Märchen *Jack the Giant Killer*; von Shakespeare in *King Lear* III, 4,183 verwendet.

14 **flurry:** Gestöber, Schwarm.

15 **Milky Way:** Milchstraße.

17 **boar:** Eber, Wildschwein.

17 f. **ratatouille:** südfranzösisches Gemüseragout.

18 **crate:** Kiste.

18 f. **une eau de vie Poire William** (Fr.): Williamsbirnenwasser, -geist.

not suggest that Raymond might swim. Raymond in fact did not like swimming; he was too fat to wish to be seen, and preferred eating and smoking. Both men drank rather a lot of red wine and then rather a lot of *eau de vie*. The smell of the mountain was laced with the smells of pork crackling and cigar smoke. Raymond peered drunkenly at Bernard's current painting. He pronounced it rather sinister, very striking, a bit weird, not quite usual, funny-coloured, a bit over the top? Looking at Bernard each time for a response and getting none, as Bernard, exhausted and a little drunk, was largely asleep. They went to bed, and Bernard woke once in the night to realise he had not shut his bedroom window as he usually did; a shutter was banging. But he was unkissed and solitary; he slid back into unconsciousness.

The next morning Bernard was up first. He made coffee, he cycled to the village and bought croissants, bread and peaches, he laid the table on the terrace and poured heated milk into a blue and white jug. The pool lay flat and still, quietly and incompatibly shining at the quiet sky.

5 **to lace:** durchsetzen, -ziehen.
6 **to crackle:** knistern.
8 **sinister:** düster.
weird: seltsam.
9 **a bit over the top** (coll.): ein bisschen verrückt.
14 **shutter:** Fensterladen.
to bang: schlagen, klappern.
15 **solitary:** einsam.
21 **incompatibly** (adv.): unvereinbar, nicht zusammenpassend.

Raymond made rather a noise coming downstairs. This was because his arm was round a young woman with a great deal of hennaed black hair, who wore a garment of that see-through cheesecloth from India which is sold in every southern French market. The garment was calf-length, clinging, with little shoulder-straps and dyed in a rather musty brownish-black, scattered with little round green spots like peas. It could have been a sundress or a nightdress; it was only too easy to see that the woman wore nothing at all underneath it. The black triangle of her pubic hair swayed with her hips. Her breasts were large and thrusting, that was the word that sprang to Bernard's mind. The nipples stood out in the cheesecloth.

"This is Melanie," Raymond announced, pulling out a chair for her. She flung back her hair with an actressy gesture of her hands and sat down gracefully, pulling the cheesecloth round her knees and staring down at her ankles. She had long pale hairless legs with very pretty feet. Her toenails were varnished with a pink pearly varnish. She turned them this way and that, admiring them. She wore rather a lot of very pink lipstick and smiled in a satisfied way at her own toes.

3 **hennaed:** mit Henna gefärbt.
4 **cheesecloth:** indischer Baumwollstoff.
6 **clinging:** eng anliegend.
7 **musty:** matt, langweilig.
11 **pubic hair:** Schambehaarung.
12 **thrusting:** nach vorn drängend, aufdringlich.
13 **nipple:** Brustwarze.
16 **to fling back:** zurückwerfen.
actressy: schauspielerinnenhaft.
20 **to varnish:** lackieren.

"Do you want coffee?" said Bernard to Melanie.

"She doesn't speak English," said Raymond. He leaned over and made a guzzling, kissing noise in the hollow of her collar-bone. "Do you, darling?"

He was obviously going to make no attempt to explain her presence. It was not even quite clear that he knew that Bernard had a right to an explanation, or that he had himself any idea where she had come from. He was simply obsessed. His fingers were pulled towards her hair like needles to a magnet: he kept standing up and kissing her breasts, her shoulders, her ears. With considerable distaste Bernard watched Raymond's fat tongue explore the coil of Melanie's ear.

"Will you have coffee?" he said to Melanie in French. He indicated the coffee pot. She bent her head towards it with a quick curving movement, sniffed it, and then hovered briefly over the milk jug.

"This," she said, indicating the hot milk. "I will drink this."

She looked at Bernard with huge black eyes under long lashes.

"I wish you joy," said Bernard in Cevenol French, "of your immortal soul."

"Hey," said Raymond, "don't flirt with my girl in foreign languages."

"I don't flirt," said Bernard. "I paint."

"And we'll be off after breakfast and leave you to your painting," said Raymond. "Won't we, my sweet dar-

3 **to guzzle:** (gierig) schlucken, schmatzen.
9 **obsessed:** besessen.
12 **distaste:** Abneigung.
17 **to hover over s.th.:** bei etwas verweilen.

ling? Melanie wants – Melanie hasn't got – she didn't exactly bring – you understand – all her clothes and things. We're going to Cannes to buy some real clothes. Melanie wants to see the film festival and the stars. You won't mind, old friend, you didn't want me in the first place. I don't want to interrupt your *painting*. *Chacun à sa boue*, as we used to say in the army, I know that much French."

Melanie held out her pretty fat hands and turned them over and over with considerable satisfaction. They were pinkly pale and also ornamented with pearly nail-varnish. She did not look at Raymond, simply twisted her head about with what could have been pleasure at his little sallies of physical affection, or could have been irritation. She did not speak. She smiled a little, over her milk, like a satisfied cat, displaying two rows of sweet little pearly teeth between her glossy pink lips.

Raymond's packing did not take long. Melanie turned out to have one piece of luggage – a large green leather bag full of rattling coins, by the sound. Raymond saw her into the car like a princess, and came back to say goodbye to his friend.

"Have a good time," said Bernard. "Beware of philosophers."

"Where would I find any philosophers?" asked Raymond, who had done theatre design at art school with

6f. **chacun à sa boue** (Fr.): Verballhornung von *chacun à son gout* ›jeder nach seinem Geschmack‹, ›jeder wie er mag‹ (*la boue:* Dreck; [fig.] [niedere] Gesinnung).

14 **sally:** Ausbruch.

20 **to rattle:** klimpern.

26 **theatre design:** Bühnenbild(nerei).

Bernard and now designed sets for a successful children's TV programme called *The A-Mazing Maze of Monsters*. "Philosophers are extinct. I think your wits are turning, old friend, with stomping around on your own. You need a girl-friend."

"I don't," said Bernard. "Have a good holiday."

"We're going to be married," said Raymond, looking surprised, as though he himself had not known this until he said it. The face of Melanie swam at the car window, the pearly teeth visible inside the soft lips, the dark eyes staring. "I must go," said Raymond. "Melanie's waiting."

Left to himself, Bernard settled back into the bliss of solitude. He looked at his latest work and saw that it was good. Encouraged, he looked at his earlier work and saw that that was good, too. All those blues, all those curious questions, all those almost-answers. The only problem was, where to go now. He walked up and down, he remembered the philosopher and laughed. He got out his Keats. He reread the dreadful moment in *Lamia* where the bride vanished away under the coldly malevolent eye of the philosopher.

2 **a-mazing:** Wortspiel mit *amazing* und *maze* ›Irrgarten, Labyrinth‹.
3 **extinct:** ausgestorben.
3 f. **your wits are turning** (arch., pl.): dein Geist dreht sich, du wirst verrückt; Anspielung auf Shakespeare, *King Lear* III,2,67.
4 **to stomp around:** herumspazieren, -walzen.
13 f. **bliss of solitude:** Glück der Einsamkeit; Zitat aus Z. 22 des Gedichts »The Daffodils« von William Wordsworth.
14 f. **saw that it was good:** Anspielung auf 1. Mose 1.
22 **malevolent:** boshaft, übelwollend.

Do not all charms fly
At the mere touch of cold philosophy?
There was an awful rainbow once in heaven:
We know her woof, her texture; she is given
In the dull catalogue of common things.
Philosophy will clip an Angel's wings,
Conquer all mysteries by rule and line,
Empty the haunted air and gnomèd mine –
Unweave a rainbow, as it erstwhile made
The tender-personed Lamia melt into a shade.

Personally, Bernard said to himself, he had never gone along with Keats about all that stuff. By philosophy Keats seemed to mean natural science, and personally he, Bernard, would rather have the optical mysteries of waves and particles in the water and light of the rainbow than any old gnome or fay. He had been at least as interested in the problems of reflection and refraction

3 **awful:** ehrfurchtgebietend, eindrucksvoll; zitiert wird aus »Lamia« II, 229–238.
4 **woof:** Gewebe.
6 **to clip:** (Flügel) stutzen.
7 **line:** Richtlinie, Grundlage, Methode, Prinzip.
8 **haunted:** von Geistern bevölkert, heimgesucht.
gnomèd (arch.): von Gnomen bevölkert.
mine: hier: Erdhöhle, unterirdische Gänge.
9 **to unweave:** entflechten, auflösen.
erstwhile (arch.): einstmalig, früher, damals.
11 f. **to go along with s.o.:** mit jdm. übereinstimmen.
15 **particle:** Teilchen.
16 **fay** (poet.): Fee.
17 **reflection:** (Licht-)Reflexion, Spiegelung.
refraction: (Licht-)Brechung.

when he had had the lovely snake in his pool as he had been in its oddity – in its *otherness* – as snakes went. He hoped no natural scientist would come along and find Melanie's blood group to be that of some sort of Herpes, or do an X-ray and see something odd in her spine. She made a very good blowzy sort of a woman, just right for Raymond. He wondered what sort of a woman she would have become for him, and dismissed the problem. He didn't want a woman. He wanted another visual idea. A mystery to be explained by rule and line. He looked around his breakfast table. A rather nondescript orange-brown butterfly was sipping the juice of the rejected peaches. It had a golden eye at the base of its wings and a rather lovely white streak, shaped like a tiny dragon-wing. It stood on the glistening rich yellow peach-flesh and manoeuvred its body to sip the sugary juices and suddenly it was not orange-brown at all, it was a rich, gleaming intense purple. And then it was both at once, orange-gold and purple-veiled, and then it was purple again, and then it folded its wings and the undersides had a purple eye

2 **oddity:** Seltsamkeit.
4 f. **herpes:** wörtl.: Kriechtier, Lurch, Reptil (von griech. *herpein* ›kriechen‹).
5 **spine:** Wirbelsäule.
6 **blowzy:** einfach, derb, schlampig.
11 f. **nondescript:** unscheinbar, undefinierbar.
12 **to sip s.th.:** an etwas nippen.
15 **dragon-wing:** Drachenflügel.
to glisten: glänzen.
18 **to gleam:** leuchten.
intense: intensiv.
19 f. **purple-veiled:** mit einem Purpurschleier.

and a soft green streak, and tan, and white edged with charcoal …

When he came back with his paintbox it was still turning and sipping. He mixed purple, he mixed orange, he made browns. It was done with a dusting of scales, with refractions of rays. The pigments were discovered and measured, the scales on the wings were noted and *seen*, everything was a mystery, serpents and water and light. He was off again. Exact study would not clip this creature's wings, it would dazzle his eyes with its brightness. Don't go, he begged it, watching and learning, don't go. Purple and orange is a terrible and violent fate. There is months of work in it. Bernard attacked it. He was happy, in one of the ways in which human beings are happy.

1 **tan:** Gelbbraun.
2 **charcoal:** Holzkohle; Kohlengrau.
10 **to dazzle:** blenden.

Editorische Notiz

Das Glossar erklärt in der Regel alle Wörter, die nicht in *Reclams Englischem Wörterbuch* von Dieter Hamblock (Stuttgart: Reclam, 1996) verzeichnet sind. Die einzelnen Short Stories sind unabhängig voneinander glossiert.

Im Glossar verwendete Abkürzungen

adv.	adverb
arch.	archaic (veraltet)
coll.	colloquial (umgangssprachlich)
fig.	figuratively (übertragen)
Fr.	French
griech.	griechisch
Lat.	Latin
o. s.	oneself
poet.	poetical (dichterisch, gehoben)
pl.	plural
s. o.	someone
s. th.	something
vulg.	vulgar (vulgär, derb)

Textnachweise

Antonia S. Byatt: A Lamia in the Cevennes. In: Christopher Hope / Peter Porter (Hrsg.): New Writing 5. London: Vintage in ass. with The British Council, 1996. S. 1–17. – Copyright © 1995 Antonia S. Byatt. Mit Genehmigung von The Peters Fraser and Dunlop Group Limited, London.

Angela Carter: The Company of Wolves. In: A. C.: The Bloody Chamber and Other Stories. Harmondsworth: Penguin, 1981. S. 110–118. Erstdruck: London: Victor Gollancz, 1979. – Copyright © 1979 Angela Carter. Mit Genehmigung von The Estate of Angela Carter c/o Rogers, Coleridge & White Ltd., London.

Penelope Fitzgerald: At Hiruharama. In: Malcolm Bradbury / Judy Cooke (Hrsg.): New Writing 1. London: Minerva in ass. with The British Council, 1992. S. 33–39. – Copyright © Penelope Fitzgerald. Mit Genehmigung der Autorin.

Nadine Gordimer: Homage. In: A. S. Byatt / Alan Hollinghurst (Hrsg.): New Writing 4. London: Vintage in ass. with The British Council, 1995. S. 404–407. – Copyright © 1995 Nadine Gordimer. Bei dem Text handelt es sich um einen Auszug aus einem längeren Werk. Mit Genehmigung von A. P. Watt Ltd. on behalf of Felix Licensing B. V., London.

Susan Hill: The Badness Within Him. In: S. H.: A Bit of Singing and Dancing. London: Hamish Hamilton, 1973. S. 161–170. – Copyright © 1971, 1972, 1973 Susan Hill. Mit Genehmigung von Sheil Land Associates Ltd., London.

Sara Maitland: The Wicked Stepmother's Tale. In: Zoë Fairbairns [u.a.] (Hrsg.): More Tales I Tell My Mother. Feminist Short Stories. London: Journeyman, 1987. S. 157–163. – Copyright © 1987 Sara Maitland. Mit Genehmigung von Pluto Press, London.

Kathy Page: It Is July, Now. In: Christopher Hope / Peter Porter (Hrsg.): New Writing 5. London: Vintage in ass. with The British Council, 1996. S. 172–183. – Copyright © 1996

Kathy Page. Mit Genehmigung von Gillon Aitken Associates Ltd., London.

Emma Tennant: Philomela. In: Malcolm Bradbury (Hrsg.): The Penguin Book of Modern British Short Stories. Harmondsworth: Penguin, 1988. S. 102–110. Erstdruck in: E. T.: »Bananas«. An Anthology, London: Quartet Books, 1977. – Copyright © 1975 Emma Tennant. Mit Genehmigung von Mohrbooks AG, Zürich.

Rose Tremain: The Beauty of the Dawn Shift. In: Christopher Hope / Peter Porter (Hrsg.): New Writing 5. London: Vintage in ass. with The British Council, 1996. S. 151–171. – Copyright © 1996 Rose Tremain. Mit Genehmigung von Sheil Land Associates Ltd., London.

Fay Weldon: In the Great War. In: F. W.: Polaris and Other Stories. London: Hodder & Stoughton, 1985. S. 129–143. – Copyright © 1985 Fay Weldon. Mit Genehmigung von Curtis Brown, Edinburgh.

Bio-bibliographische Überblicke

ANTONIA SUSAN BYATT

Geb. am 24. August 1936 in Sheffield. Byatt studierte Englisch am Newnham College, Cambridge; weiteres Studium in Pennsylvania und Oxford. Dann unterrichtete sie an der Central School of Art and Design und am University College in London. Seit 1983 widmet sie sich ganz ihrer schriftstellerischen Arbeit.
In einem Interview erklärte Byatt 1982, daß sie eher in der Tradition von Henry James, T. S. Eliot und Ezra Pound stehe als in einer Tradition von SchriftstellerInnen. »Literature has always been my way out, my escape from the limits of being female.« Bekannt wurde sie einem großen Lesepublikum vor allem durch ihren 1990 erschienenen Roman *Possession: A Romance*, für den sie den Booker Prize erhielt, die renommierteste Auszeichnung für englische Gegenwartserzählliteratur. Byatt ist auch als Kritikerin, als Mitglied des PEN-Clubs und als Vorsitzende der britischen Society of Authors hervorgetreten. Sie ist Mutter von drei Töchtern und lebt in London.

Werke: *Shadow of a Sun* (1964); *The Game* (1967); *The Virgin in the Garden* (1978); *Still Life* (1985); *Sugar and Other Stories* (1987); *Possession: A Romance* (1990); *Passions of the Mind: Selected Writings* (1991); *Angels and Insects* (1992); *The Matisse Stories* (1993); *Babel Tower* (1996).

Sekundärliteratur: Kathleen Coyne Kelly, *A. S. Byatt*, New York 1996 (Twayne's English Authors Series); Richard Todd, *A. S. Byatt*, Plymouth 1997 (Writers and Their Work).

ANGELA CARTER

Geb. am 17. Mai 1940. Carter wuchs in Yorkshire und London auf, studierte Englisch an der Universität Bristol und verbrachte danach zwei Jahre in Japan. 1976–78 lehrte sie Creative Writing an der Universität Sheffield und 1980/81 an der Brown University, Long Island. Nach längerem Aufenthalt in den USA kehrte sie nach Großbritannien zurück und starb, erst 51-jährig, am 16. Februar 1992 in London.
Während ihres Studiums spezialisierte Carter sich auf mittelalterliche Literatur und entwickelte ein besonderes Interesse an Mythen und Folklore. Anthropologie, Soziologie und Psychologie zählten ebenfalls zu ihren Studien- und Interessensgebieten.
Nach eigenen Aussagen betrachtet sie konventionelles mimetisches Erzählen als eine Form eskapistischer Wirklichkeitsvermeidung aller unheimlichen oder ambivalenten Phänomene. Sie ist eine literarische Bilderstürmerin im Zeitalter der Dekonstruktion. Binäre Oppositionen lösen sich ihrer Meinung nach auf; so sagt sie z. B.: »The whole notion of the ›natural‹ is an invention of culture anyway«. Wirklichkeit vs. Phantasie, Kultur vs. Natur, Gut vs. Böse, Barbarei vs. Zivilisation – alle klaren Gegensätze werden überwunden oder transformiert. Von Carters Werken hat die Short-Story-Sammlung *The Bloody Chamber* besondere Berühmtheit erlangt. Die Erzählungen sind thematisch miteinander verbunden und meist Nach-Erzählungen von Mythen und Märchen. Sie gewann dafür den Cheltenham Festival of Literature Award. Carters Gesamtwerk hat bereits einen beträchtlichen Nachhall auf Seiten der Literaturkritik erfahren.

Werke: *Shadow Dance* (1966); *The Magic Toyshop* (1967); *Several Perceptions* (1968); *Heroes and Villains* (1969); *Love: A Novel* (1971); *The Infernal Desire Machines of Doctor Hoffman: A Novel* (1972); *The Passion of New Eve* (1977); *The Bloody Chamber, and Other Stories* (1979); *The Sadeian Woman: An Exercise in Cultural History* (1979); *Black Venus's*

Tale (1980); *Nothing Sacred* (Essays) (1982); *Nights at the Circus* (1984); *Wise Children* (1992); *Burning Your Boats: The Collected Short Stories* (1996).

Sekundärliteratur: Joseph Bristow (Hrsg.), *The Infernal Desires of Angela Carter: Fiction, Femininity, Feminism*, London 1997 (Studies in Twentieth Century Literature); Sarah Gamble, *Angela Carter: Writing from the Frontier*, Edinburgh 1997; Anne Koenen, »Vampire of the Senses: The Feminist Fantastic of Angela Carter«, in: *anglistik & englischunterricht* 59 (1996) S. 143–162; Alison Lee, *Angela Carter*, New York 1997 (Twayne's English Authors Series); Anja Müller, *Angela Carter: Identity Constructed, Deconstructed*, Heidelberg 1997; Linden Peach, *Angela Carter*, New York 1997; Ingrid von Rosenberg, »Angela Carter: Mistress of Voices«, in: *(Sub)Versions of Realism – Recent Women's Fiction in Britain*, hrsg. von Irmgard Maassen und Anna Maria Stuby, Heidelberg: Winter, 1997 (*anglistik & englischunterricht*, 60); Lorna Sage (Hrsg.), *Flesh and the Mirror: Essays on the Art of Angela Carter*, London 1994; Lorna Sage, *Angela Carter*, Plymouth 1996 (Writers and Their Work); Lindsey Tucker (Hrsg.), *Critical Essays on Angela Carter*, New York 1998.

PENELOPE FITZGERALD

Geb. am 17. Dezember 1916 in Lincoln. Fitzgerald studierte Englisch am Somerville College, Oxford, und wurde Lehrerin. 1979 erhielt sie den Booker Prize, nachdem sie Kurzromane veröffentlicht hatte. »I like economy and compression« ist Fitzgeralds Begründung für die Bevorzugung der Kurzprosa in ihrer schriftstellerischen Arbeit.

Werke (Auswahl): *Offshore* (1979); *Human Voices* (1982); *Innocence* (1986); *The Beginning of Spring* (1990); *The Gate of Angels* (1991); *The Blue Flower* (1995).

Sekundärliteratur: Edward Burne Jones, *Penelope Fitzgerald*, Stroud 1997.

NADINE GORDIMER

Geb. am 20. November 1923 in Transvaal als Tochter eines jüdischen Uhrmachers, der mit seiner englischen Ehefrau aus dem Baltikum nach Südafrika ausgewandert war. Mit neun Jahren begann Gordimer zu schreiben. Sie besuchte die Witwatersrand Universität in Johannesburg und engagierte sich innerlich mehr und mehr für eine multikulturelle Gesellschaft in Südafrika. D. H. Lawrence, Henry James und Ernest Hemingway waren ihre literarischen Vorbilder. 1991 wurde sie mit dem Nobelpreis für Literatur ausgezeichnet.

Werke (Auswahl): *Occasion for Loving* (1963); *A Guest of Honour* (1971); *The Conservationist* (1974); *Burger's Daughter* (1979); *A Sport of Nature* (1987); *My Son's Story* (1990); *Jump* (Kurzgeschichtensammlung) (1991); *None to Accompany Me* (1994); *The House Gun* (1997).

Sekundärliteratur: *Ariel* 19 (1988), H. 4 [Sonderheft zu Nadine Gordimer]; Stephen Clingman, *The Novels of Nadine Gordimer*, Oxford 1986; John W. Cooke, *The Novels of Nadine Gordimer: Private Lives, Public Landscapes*; Baton Rouge 1985; Antje Hagena, *Nadine Gordimers neuere Romane: Eine Untersuchung in Thematik und Erzählstrategie*, Essen 1987; Dominic Head, *Nadine Gordimer*, Cambridge 1994 (Cambridge Studies in African and Caribbean Literature, 2); Bruce King (Hrsg.), *The Later Fiction of Nadine Gordimer*, London 1993; Klaus Kreimeier, *Nadine Gordimer*, München 1991; Liliane Louvel, *Nadine Gordimer*, Nancy 1994; Judie Newman, *Nadine Gordimer*, London / New York 1988 (Contemporary Writers); Rowland Smith, *Critical Essays on Nadine Gordimer*, Boston 1990 (Critical Essays on World Literature Series); Barbara Temple-Thurston, *Nadine Gordimer Revisited*, New York 1999 (Twayne's World Authors Series, 881); Kathrin M. Wagner, *Rereading Nadine Gordimer*, Bloomington 1994.

SUSAN HILL

Geb. am 5. Februar 1942 in Scarborough (Yorkshire). Hill besuchte die Grammar School und studierte Englisch am King's College in London. Seit vielen Jahren arbeitet sie hauptberuflich als Schriftstellerin, verfasste jedoch auch zahlreiche Kolumnen und Rezensionen für Zeitungen. Hill war »Fellow« am King's College und erhielt eine Reihe von literarischen Auszeichnungen.

Werke: *A Bit of Singing and Dancing* (1973); *In the Springtime of the Year* (1974); *The Bird of Night* (1976); *A Change for the Better* (1980); *The Albatross and Other Stories* (1982); *Ghost Stories* (1983); *The Woman in Black* (1984); *Listening to the Orchestra: Four Stories* (1996).

Sekundärliteratur: Ernest H. Hofer, »Enclosed Structures, Disclosed Lives: The Fictions of Susan Hill«, in: E. H. H.: *Contemporary British Women Writers. Texts and Strategies*, London 1993, S. 128–150; Rosemary Jackson, »Cold Enclosures: The Fiction of Susan Hill«, in: Thomas F. Staley (Hrsg.), *Twentieth-Century Women Novelists*, London 1982, S. 81–103; Barbara Keller, *Woman's Journey Toward Self and Its Literary Exploration*, Bern 1986; Kenneth Muir, »Susan Hill's Fiction«, in: Douglas Jefferson / Graham Martin (Hrsg.), *The Uses of Fiction: Essays on the Modern Novel in Honour of Arnold Kettle*, Milton Keynes 1982, S. 273–285.

SARA MAITLAND

Geb. 1950. Maitland strebte zunächst eine Laufbahn als Predigerin an und befasst sich in Erzählprosa und Non-Fiction auch jetzt noch häufig mit religiösen Themen.

Werke: *Telling Tales: Short Stories* (1983); (Hrsg., zus. mit Aileen La Tourette) *Weddings and Funerals* (Short Stories)

(1984); *Women Fly when Men aren't Watching: Short Stories* (1993); *Home Truths* (1994); *Angel and Me: Short Stories for Holy Week* (1995).

KATHY PAGE

Geb. 1958. Page lebt in London und ist im sozialpsychologischen Beratungsdienst tätig. Bis jetzt hat sie vier Romane und eine Short-Story-Sammlung veröffentlicht; ihre Erzählungen sind auch häufig in Anthologien abgedruckt worden.

Werke: *Back in the First Person* (1986); *The Unborn Dreams of Clara Riley* (1987); *Island Paradise* (1989); *As in Music: Stories* (1990); *Frankie Styne and the Silver Man* (1992).

EMMA TENNANT

Geb. 1937 in London. Tennant wuchs in ländlicher Umgebung auf, studierte kurz Kunstgeschichte in Paris und fing dann als Kolumnistin an, für Zeitungen in England zu schreiben; sie gründete 1975 die Zeitschrift *Bananas,* in der neue Literatur veröffentlicht wurde. »Black humour« und Satire sind ihre Hauptausdrucksformen, Fantasy und Meta-Fiktion ihre Lieblingsgenres, wobei sie häufig ein »re-writing« von literarischen Texten betreibt. Tennant lebt mit ihren drei Kindern in London.

Werke: *Hotel de Dream* (1978); *The Crack* (1978); *Woman Beware Woman* (1984); *The Ghost Child* (1984); *The Adventures of Robina, by herself: Being the Memoirs of a Debutante at the Court of Queen Elizabeth II* (1987); *Two Women of London: The Strange Case of Ms. Jekyll and Mrs. Hyde* (1989); *The Magic Drum* (1989); *Sisters and Strangers: A Moral Tale* (1990); *Faustine* (1992); *Travesties* (1995).

Sekundärliteratur: Olga Kenyon, *Women Writers Talk. Interviews with 10 Women Writers*, Oxford 1989, S. 173–187; Susanne Schmid, »Emma Tennant's Sister Hyde: Two Strange Cases of the Female Double«, in: *Zeitschrift für Anglistik und Amerikanistik* 45 (1997), H. 1, S. 20–32; Emma Tennant, *Emma Tennant with James Buxton*, London 1987.

ROSE TREMAIN

Geb. 1943. Tremain studierte an der University of East Anglia in Norwich. Dort lehrt sie Creative Writing und schreibt literarkritische Rezensionen für Presse und Rundfunk. Ihre schriftstellerische Tätigkeit umfasst Romane, Kurzgeschichten und Hörspiele sowie Drehbücher für Fernsehverfilmungen.
Rose Tremains ›Credo‹ als Autorin beinhaltet, dass das Ungewöhnliche das Gewohnte in einem neuen Licht erscheinen lässt und dass das Gegenwärtige durch die historisch gewordenen Erfahrungen erhellt wird. Diese Parameter kennzeichnen ihr literarisches Werk, das mit einem Schlag bekannt wurde, als Tremains Roman *Restoration* 1989 in die engere Wahl für den renommierten Booker Prize kam; in ihm wird besonders die Bedeutung der Vergangenheit für die Gegenwart thematisiert.
Rezensenten und Kritiker heben an Tremains Werken stets ihren trockenen Humor und ihre scharfsinnige Ironie hervor. Sie scheut jedoch auch vor noch bestehenden thematischen Tabus (Geisteskrankheit, Erotisierung von Macht, Geschlechtsumwandlung) und vor drastischen Darstellungen nicht zurück.

Werke: *Sadler's Birthday* (1976); *Letter to Sister Benedicta* (1978); *The Cupboard* (1981); *The Colonel's Daughter and Other Stories* (1984); *Journey to the Volcano* (1985); *The Swimming Pool Season* (1985); *The Garden of the Villa Mollini and Other Stories* (1987); *Restoration* (1989); *Sacred Country* (1992); *The Way I Found Her* (1998).

Sekundärliteratur: Birgit Moosmüller, *Die experimentelle englische Kurzgeschichte der Gegenwart*, München 1993.

FAY WELDON

Geb. am 22. September 1933 in Alvechurch (Worcestershire). Weldon wuchs in Neuseeland bei ihrer Mutter, Großmutter und Schwester auf und gewann den Eindruck, »[that] the world was peopled by females«. Sie kehrte nach Großbritannien zurück und studierte an der Universität von St. Andrews in Schottland Wirtschaftswissenschaften und Psychologie. Anschließend arbeitete sie als Werbetexterin, heiratete und bekam vier Söhne.
Ihre literarische Karriere begann in den sechziger Jahren mit einer großen Anzahl von Fernsehspielen, Hörspielen und Bühnenstücken. 1967 erschien ihr erster Roman, und fortan wurde Erzählliteratur ihre Hauptdomäne. Feminismus und die Beziehungen von Frauen zueinander sind Weldons thematische Schwerpunkte, Satire und Polemik die wichtigsten Ausdrucksformen ihrer schriftstellerischen Arbeit.

Werke (Auswahl): *The Fat Woman's Joke* (1967); *Down Among the Women* (1971); *Female Friends* (1975); *Praxis* (1978); *Puffball* (1980); *Watching Me, Watching You* (Short Stories) (1981); *The President's Child* (1982); *The Life and Loves of a She-Devil* (1984); *Polaris and Other Stories* (1985); *The Shrapnel Academy* (1986); *The Cloning of Joanna May* (1989); *Moon over Minneapolis* (Short Stories) (1991); *Trouble* (1993); *Worst Fears* (1996).

Sekundärliteratur: Susanne Becker, »The Haunted Voices of Fay Weldon«, in: *anglistik & englischunterricht* 48 (1992) S. 99–113; Elfi Bettinger / Helene Decke-Cornill; »Lakonisch und lebensklug. Ein Gespräch mit Fay Weldon«, in: *Hard Times. Deutsch-englische Zeitschrift* 40 (1990) S. 10–13; Finuala Dowling, *Fay Weldon's Fiction*, London 1998; Laura Faulks, *Fay Weldon*, New York 1998 (Twayne's English Authors Series); Olga Kenyon, *Women Novelists Today: A Survey of English Writing in the Seventies and Eighties*, Brighton 1988; Barbara Puschmann-Nalenz, »Cloudy Symbols of a (not so)

High Romance«, in: *anglistik & englischunterricht* 59 (1996) S. 163–180; Barbara Puschmann-Nalenz (Hrsg.), »Nachwort«, in: *Fay Weldon, The Fat Woman's Joke*, Stuttgart 1996; Wolfgang Riedel, »Fay Weldon's ›Weekend‹: Eine Geschichte von der subversiven Ironie des Glücks«, in: *anglistik & englischunterricht* 50 (1993) S. 55–65; Lorna Sage, *Women in the House of Fiction: Post-War Women Novelists*, New York / London 1992; Patricia Waugh, *Feminine Fictions: Revisiting the Postmodern*, London 1989; Alan Wilde, »Bold, but not too Bold: Fay Weldon and the Limits of Poststructuralist Criticism«, in: *Contemporary Literature* 29 (1988) S. 403–419.

Literaturhinweise allgemein zur Short Story

Bonheim, Helmut, *The Narrative Modes: Techniques of the Short Story*, Neuaufl. Cambridge 1986.

Broich, Ulrich, »Muted Postmodernism: The Contemporary British Short Story«, in: *Zeitschrift für Anglistik und Amerikanistik* 41 (1993), H. 1, S. 31–39.

Lubbers, Klaus (Hrsg.), *Die englische und amerikanische Kurzgeschichte*, Darmstadt 1990.

Recent British Short Story Writing, hrsg. von Hans-Jürgen Diller, Heidelberg: Winter, 1993 (*anglistik & englischunterricht*, 50).

Shaw, Valerie, *The Short Story: A Critical Introduction*, London 1983.

Nachwort

Zur Auswahl der Short Stories

Die Auswahl der vorliegenden Short Stories scheint homogen und gleichzeitig disparat. Während alle Texte von in Großbritannien veröffentlichenden und mit Ausnahme der früh verstorbenen Angela Carter noch lebenden Autorinnen verfasst wurden, sind Themen und Erzähltechniken und sogar die bei der Short Story gattungsprägende Länge ganz verschieden. Die Texte repräsentieren die wichtigsten Strömungen der Short Fiction in den vergangenen fünfundzwanzig Jahren und darüber hinaus sehr wesentliche Entwicklungen der Prosaliteratur insgesamt. Darin unterscheiden sie sich kaum von Short Stories der männlichen Kollegen. Einige der Erzählungen tragen feministische Markierungen, andere hingegen, zumindest scheinbar, gar nicht.
Im Folgenden möchte ich zunächst die vorliegenden Short Stories thematisch gruppieren, um einige Trends zeitgenössischer Kurzgeschichtenprosa zu verdeutlichen.
Das Thema der Grenzüberschreitung wird in unterschiedlicher Weise aktualisiert. Die am frühesten entstandene Short Story von Susan Hill befasst sich mit der Grenze eines Lebensabschnitts: dem Eintritt in die Adoleszenz, »Homage« von Nadine Gordimer hingegen mit Grenzverletzungen von Normen und Geboten und mit der Überschreitung der Grenze zum Tod. Das tut auch Rose Tremain, die dieses Thema außerdem ganz wörtlich als »Grenzübertritt« zur Sprache bringt. Doch ist Tremains Zeitwende-Erzählung vor allem ein Beispiel für historiographische Fiktion, »Geschichte von unten«, die auch eine Revision der Geschichtschronik der Sieger und Herrschenden ist – hier liegt die Geschichte der Unterlegenen und Ohnmächtigen vor uns, ein »Wehe den Besiegten!« anstelle des dominierenden Jubels der Befreiten – oder der Befreier! Bei Tremain findet diese Negativperspektive

einen vielschichtigen Ausdruck. Interessant ist dabei, dass die Perspektive der Diskriminierten hier nicht in erster Linie die einer Frau ist, wie so oft in der von Frauen während der letzten Jahrzehnte verfassten Prosaliteratur; vielmehr ist es die eines Mannes, der in politischer, weltanschaulicher und sexueller Hinsicht falsch liegt. Generell gilt für die vorliegenden Short Stories, dass vehementer Feminismus, wie in den siebziger Jahren verbreitet, hier Seltenheitswert besitzt; selbst Fay Weldons »In the Great War« schreibt eher eine Chronik der vorfeministischen und beginnenden feministischen Epoche und stellt am Schluss beides ausdrücklich als vorübergehende Abschnitte dar.

Eine ganz wesentliche Richtung des *fiction-writing* zeichnet sich in der 1975 von Emma Tennant veröffentlichten Geschichte »Philomela« ab, die zwar eine feministische Botschaft enthält, deren stärkster Nachdruck aber auf der Neufassung eines existenten Textes, des antiken Mythos, liegt. Dies ist umso bemerkenswerter, als mehr als zwanzig Jahre später Antonia S. Byatt noch immer das »re-writing« von mythologischen Texten betreibt. In einem Auswahl- und Modifikationsprozess, »choosing among fictions«, schreibt Angela Carter einen neuen Text aus mehreren alten und nennt ihn »The Company of Wolves«; er erschien in einer ganzen Anthologie von Carters Nach-Erzählungen von Märchen und Mythen. Sara Maitland hingegen erzählt monologisch das Aschenputtel-Märchen neu aus einer heterogenen Perspektive. Während der antike und der mündlich überlieferte Mythos überindividuell von einem weit entfernten Erzählerstandpunkt aus entwickelt werden, nehmen diese Nach-Erzählungen eine personale oder Ich-Erzählsituation auf.

Schließlich sind noch die Erzählungen mit der Thematik des »Fremden« oder »Ausländers« zu nennen, die beide in eine feministische Aussage münden und in den neunziger Jahren publiziert wurden: In »At Hiruharama« und »It is July, Now« treten Frauen in den Vordergrund und werden zu den wichtigsten Personen in einer männlich dominierten Welt.

Die Erzählstrategien weisen eine ebenso starke Diversifikation auf wie die Themen der Short Stories: Zu jedem Zeitpunkt im Zeitalter der Postmoderne wird die Fiktion durch konservative und durch experimentelle Schreibweisen vertreten, mimetische steht neben nichtmimetisch-fantastischer Literatur, realistische Erzählkonventionen sind gleichzeitig mit postmodernen repräsentiert. Der gewagteste Text im Sinn avantgardistischen Schreibens ist der von Angela Carter, doch auch Antonia S. Byatt experimentiert fröhlich mit der Postmoderne. Diese ist sowohl ein Epochen- als auch ein Stilbegriff, der sämtliche Aspekte des Schreibens und der Künste umfassen kann. Im Zeitalter der Postmoderne, in dem wir leben, beteiligen sich nicht alle Autorinnen am Dekonstruieren und Rekonfigurieren; etliche fahren auch fort auf der Linie etablierter Erzählkonventionen und vertrauter Wirklichkeitsperzeption.

Zu den einzelnen Short Stories

Susan Hill, »The Badness Within Him« (1973)

Die früheste der hier anthologisierten Erzählungen stellt ein Beispiel vom Typus »Initiationsgeschichte« dar. Mit »Initiation« ist der Übertritt vom Kindes- zum Adoleszenz- bzw. Erwachsenenalter gemeint. Diese entscheidende Phase im Leben eines Individuums gehört zu den häufig bearbeiteten Themen der Erzählprosa; eines der bekanntesten Werke stellt Jerome D. Salingers Roman *The Catcher in the Rye* (1951) dar. Als Beispiel für eine Short Story mit Initiationsthematik sei Doris Lessings »Through the Tunnel« (1954 erstmals veröffentlicht; später in den Band *The Habit of Loving*, 1957, aufgenommen)[1] genannt. Beide Werke haben,

1 Sie ist z. B. in folgender Sammlung abgedruckt: *Modern English Short Stories III. From Bates to Swift*, hrsg. von Hans-Christian Oeser, Stuttgart: Reclam, 1986, S. 52-67 (Universal-Bibliothek, 9202).

wie zahlreiche Initiationserzählungen, einen männlichen Protagonisten.

In Susan Hills Short Story ist es Col[in]; wie der Leser aus dem Text erschließen kann, ist er elf oder zwölf Jahre alt: »Jess [seine Schwester] looked up slowly. This year, for the first time, Col felt the difference in age between them, he saw that Jess was changing, moving away from him to join the adults. She was almost fourteen« (S. 5). Die Einzelheiten über Cols Familie und Lebenszuschnitt lässt der Erzähler beiläufig in die Geschichte einfließen und macht dadurch deutlich, dass die Gewichtungen anders verteilt sind als beispielsweise bei einem Lebenslauf. Die Erzählung führt nämlich im ersten Abschnitt unvermittelt das Thema der Überschrift ein: Col fühlt sich »schlecht«, böse, aufbegehrend, und das ohne plausible Erklärung. Er befindet sich auf einer Ferienreise am Meer, wo er Jahr für Jahr mit seinen Eltern und Geschwistern den Sommerurlaub verbringt.

Diese Routine wird unterbrochen durch Cols Eintritt in eine entscheidende innere Entwicklung, deren Inhalt und Bedeutung von ihm selbst aber – wie später der Tod des Vaters – nicht klar eingeordnet werden können. Er hegt Groll gegen seine Eltern und Geschwister und ist unzufrieden mit den Ferien. Alles, was ihm bisher so gut gefallen hat, ist für ihn jetzt störend, ja, mitunter unerträglich. Er hasst alles und empfindet sich deshalb als innerlich schlecht. Die Geschichte beginnt damit, dass er um ein Gewitter betet, damit endlich der ewige Sonnenschein aufhören möge und sich wenigstens am Wetter etwas ändert, wenn sonst schon alles so bleibt, wie es immer war, und sie endet mit der Erkenntnis, »that the change had come [...], and that his childhood had ended too, that they would never come to this house again« (S. 19). Cols Abneigung gegen den Ferienort und alles, was sich damit verbindet, macht die Abkehr vom Lebensabschnitt der Kindheit deutlich.

Seine »Schlechtigkeit« wird von ihm selbst aber auf kindliche Art und Weise magisch interpretiert: Am Schluss der Erzählung fühlt er, dass er schuldig ist am Tod seines Vaters, der vor seinen Augen, aber unerreichbar fern von ihm, im Meer ertrunken ist. Schuldig, weil die Macht seiner Schlechtigkeit so groß ist, dass sie den Tod des Vaters »bewirken« konnte (»it is my fault«, S. 17). Das magische Denken im Unterschied zum Kausalitätsprinzip charakterisiert Col noch als Kind; mit dem Tod des Vaters aber hört die Kindheit definitiv auf.

Denn der Vater ist Rollenvorbild; von ihm kann sich der heranwachsende Sohn abgrenzen, mit ihm kann er rivalisieren oder sich identifizieren. Doch Cols Beziehung zum Vater bleibt ungeklärt und distanziert: »Col said, do I like my father? And thought about it. And did not know« (S. 15). Von seinem »family circle« (S. 10), der aus seiner Mutter, den beiden älteren Schwestern Jess und Fay und Fays Baby besteht, sucht er bewusst Distanz, weil diese ihn stören, gängeln und kritisieren. Bezeichnenderweise kommt der Vater nur am Wochenende »zu Besuch« aus London, wo er sich beruflich aufhält; d. h. noch lebt Col ganz in der »domestic world«, zusammen mit Frauen und kleinen Kindern. Sein Vater, der die Welt des Mannes und die Erwachsenenwelt – Arbeiten und Geldverdienen – verkörpert, weckt widersprüchliche Gefühle, was sich vor allem in der Schilderung seines fremdartigen Äußeren widerspiegelt (»hairy and thickly fleshed, to lie on a rug and snore«, S. 10). Cols Ambivalenz resultiert daraus, dass er sich in einem Zwischenstadium befindet. Er steht an der Grenze zwischen zwei Lebensabschnitten, zwischen Zugehörigkeit und Trennung, zwischen Gehorsam und Aufbegehren, Liebe und Hass. Die Familie sieht er, ebenso wie den Tod des Vaters, als unbeteiligter Beobachter buchstäblich aus der Ferne, von der Höhe der Klippen, auf die er sich zurückgezogen hat.

Die Short Story behandelt in konservativem Erzählstil ein literarisches Motiv, das in der Literatur des 20. Jahrhunderts vielfach variiert worden ist. Trotz des auktorialen Erzählers folgt der Leser weitgehend der Perspektive des Protagonisten, dessen Umwelt und Erleben er allerdings abweichend von diesem interpretieren wird: Wenn Col Schuld fühlt (»I am filled with evil, there is no hope for me«, S. 13), wird der (erwachsene) Leser dies wohl als Anzeichen für einen der starken Konflikte deuten, die das Überschreiten der Schwelle zum Erwachsenwerden üblicherweise begleiten, so dass Col, objektiv betrachtet, keineswegs böser ist als andere. Er hat den Tod des Vaters nicht verursacht, noch nicht einmal definitiv gewünscht, aber er hat ihm tatenlos zugesehen, und er hat ablehnende Gefühle für seinen Vater gehegt.

Emma Tennant, »Philomela« (1975)

Philomela wird zwar zur Heldin der Erzählung, aber ihre Schwester Prokne ist die Ich-Erzählerin. Der erste Satz allerdings stellt dieses Verhältnis noch anders dar: Vor Proknes Heirat ist Philomela die Beredtere, die die Gedanken beider zu artikulieren vermag.
Die Artikulation von Gefühlen und Gedanken wird denn auch zu einem thematischen Schwerpunkt der Geschichte; in ihrem Verlauf verstummt Philomela jedoch und findet erst am Schluss neue Wege, sich mitzuteilen.
Im Gegensatz zu Philomela ist Prokne meist stumm – sowohl vor als auch während ihrer Ehe, bis zum Racheakt, mit dem sie und ihre Schwester den zügellosen Tereus bestrafen. Die abschließenden Worte zu ihrem Gemahl: »You destroyed us long ago« – markant in einer Erzählung, die sich kaum der wörtlichen Rede bedient –, weisen auf die Bedeutung des Sprechens bzw. Verstummens hin. Philomela nämlich wird stumm gemacht durch den Mann ihrer Schwester. Als Extrem des Verstummens kann der Tod gelten; Philomela sei tot, sagt daher Tereus seiner Frau, als er nach Hause zurückkehrt, und deshalb könne er sie nicht, wie versprochen, mitbringen. Doch gänzlich konnte er sie nicht zum Verstummen bringen. Philomela lebt und teilt Prokne später auf andere Weise als durch Worte, nämlich durch die Bilder eines selbstgefertigten Teppichs, mit, was ihr widerfuhr: Tereus hat sie vergewaltigt und ihr die Zunge herausgeschnitten, damit sie das schreckliche

Geschehen nicht weitererzählen kann. Als Philomela schließlich zu ihrer Schwester zurückkehrt, kann sie sich auch durch Augenkontakt verständlich machen. Stumm nimmt sie Rache, »like the priestess of an oracle without a voice« (S. 33): Gemeinsam mit Prokne tötet sie deren Sohn Itylus und setzt ihn seinem Vater Tereus als Mahl vor.

Die Short Story stellt das erste Beispiel der vorliegenden Sammlung für das »re-writing« eines bereits existierenden Textes dar, dessen früheste überlieferte Version in Ovids *Metamorphosen* (6,424-674) steht. Dort hat sie ein versöhnliches Ende, weil Prokne, Philomela und Tereus in Singvögel verwandelt werden. Dieser Schluss fehlt jedoch in der Nach-Erzählung. Ein weiterer wesentlicher Unterschied der Textvorlage besteht darin, dass Tereus, der seine Frau aufs Land schickt, weil er sich in Philomela verliebt hat, diese überzeugt, dass Prokne tot sei; nur so gelingt es ihm, Philomela gewaltlos zu verführen. Bis auf diese beiden Abweichungen folgt Emma Tennants Short Story Ovids *Metamorphosen*-Erzählung erstaunlich dicht, wenn man den langen Zeitraum bedenkt, der zwischen dem lateinischen Text und der englischen Kurzgeschichte liegt. Nun erfreuen sich natürlich antike Stoffe aus Dichtung und Mythologie großer Beliebtheit in der Moderne,[2] doch das vorliegende Beispiel ist in seiner Art neu; übrigens finden sich die meisten modernen Bearbeitungen antiker Texte in der Gattung Drama.

Emma Tennant jedoch ist eine der Autorinnen, die von den Mythen zu neuen Werken der Prosaliteratur inspiriert werden. Der Mythos hat sowohl in der Literatur als auch in der Literaturwissenschaft und Philosophie der zweiten Hälfte des 20. Jahrhunderts großen Widerhall gefunden, und zwar in Europa ebenso wie in den USA (Leslie Fiedler und Northrop Frye). Seit etwa 1970 haben sich Strukturalismus und Anthropologie der Mythenforschung besonders angenommen.

2 Vgl. hierzu Susanne Schmid, »Mythomaniacs: Contemporary Women Writers and Their Use of Myth«, in: *Anglistentag 1996 Dresden – Proceedings*, hrsg. von Uwe Böker [u. a.], Trier 1997, S. 363–371.

Mythen, so gemeinhin die Kurzdefinition, drücken die Riten, Werte und Sanktionen eines Kollektivs aus, das seine kulturelle Identität durch sie festigt und tradiert; im vorliegenden Textbeispiel geht es um das barbarische Verbrechen an einer Frau, das nur durch ein anderes barbarisches Verbrechen gesühnt werden kann. Das Motiv kannibalistischer Eltern ist in der griechischen Mythologie, die vielfach auch Ovids Dichtungen zugrunde liegt, öfters zu finden (z.B. Kronos, der seine Kinder mit Ausnahme von Zeus verschlingt; Medea, die dem verräterischen Jason seine eigenen Kinder als Mahlzeit vorsetzt). Diese Art von Rache scheint dem heutigen Leser als Sanktion für Ehebruch womöglich abstrus, und die Erforschung des Kannibalismusmotivs würde eine eigene Studie erforderlich machen. Auf der Hand liegt hingegen die Bedeutung der Tat für den Bestraften selbst; der Mann wird dadurch geschändet, dass seine Nachkommenschaft von ihm selbst unwissentlich vernichtet wird.
Im Hinblick auf das archaische Motiv des Vaters, der seine Söhne verschlingt, stellt sich die Frage, was an Tennants Nacherzählung des Mythos von Prokne, Philomela und Tereus zeitgenössisch ist. Modern erweisen sich vor allem die feministische Komponente und die Solidarität der beiden Frauen, die hier auch im wörtlichen Sinne eine »sisterhood« bilden. Die Rache für die Schmähung der Frau, ihre körperliche und seelische Verletzung, ist in dem antiken Stoff bereits so barbarisch wie in der vorliegenden Erzählung. Diese wird hier noch zusätzlich motiviert durch die Ähnlichkeit, die Itylus bereits als Knabe mit seinem Vater Tereus besitzt: seine männliche Herrschsucht, sein arrogantes Imponiergehabe.
Den furchtbaren Details der Rache entsprechen die furchtbaren Leiden Philomelas, aber auch Proknes, die unter Kälte, Isolation und der Gefühllosigkeit ihres Gemahls leidet und nur bei ihrer Schwester den seelischen Gleichklang zu finden glaubt, der ihr aus ihrem metaphorischen Gefängnis hilft; Philomela hingegen wird von ihr aus der wörtlichen Gefangenschaft befreit, in die Tereus sie gebracht hat.

Ein weiteres Element, das Aufmerksamkeit verdient, ist die suggestive Metaphorik der Short Story, insbesondere die deiktische räumliche Umgebung.

Angela Carter, »The Company of Wolves« (1979)

Carter liefert ein zweites und das wahrscheinlich bekannteste Beispiel für das »re-writing« mythologischer Stoffe; Volkssage und Märchen bilden die Textvorlage für diese Short Story, die erstmals in der Sammlung *The Bloody Chamber* erschien, zusammen mit anderen modernen Sagenfassungen wie z. B. der vom Erlkönig.

Die Erzählung stellt eine Textcollage dar, die eine Reihe von Ausgangstexten be- und verarbeitet: Der verbreitetste und umfangreichste ist der des »Rotkäppchen«-Märchens; ihm gehen eine kürzere und eine längere Werwolf-Geschichte voran, die in Form einer Klimax in die Serie von Textabschnitten über den Wolf eingeschoben sind. Beide Werwolf-Erzählungen haben einen deutlich erkennbaren Anfang und Schluss; das Ende wird durch den Tod des Werwolfs bzw. durch seine Metamorphose zum Menschen markiert, der Anfang durch die märchentypischen unbestimmten Zeitangaben »once« (S. 38) und »Not so very long ago« (S. 39). Letztere ist zwar in ihrer Verneinung untypisch, stellt aber dennoch eine Variante des Märchenanfangs dar.

Die drei in sich geschlossenen Binnenerzählungen basieren unverkennbar auf ihren Prä-Texten, wandeln sie jedoch so stark ab, dass sowohl Botschaft als auch vermittelte Werte eine Veränderung erfahren. Dies zeigt sich bei der »Rotkäppchen«-Geschichte am deutlichsten; die Protagonistin befindet sich auf der Schwelle vom Kind zum jungen Mädchen, sie ist weniger das brave Geschöpf als ein unternehmungslustiges und neugieriges Wesen. Wolf und Jäger sind ein- und dieselbe Person, die sich vom Mann in ein wildes Tier verwandelt und umgekehrt. Am Schluss schläft Rotkäppchen friedlich zusammen mit dem gezähmten Wolf im

Bett der getöteten Großmutter »in a savage marriage ceremony« (S. 56).

Wie unschwer an diesen Beispielen zu erkennen ist, impliziert die Nach-Erzählung bereits eine psychoanalytische Deutung, die als Subtext fungiert. Sicherlich kann man die Ansicht vertreten, dass der Rotkäppchen-Text dadurch überdeterminiert wird, d.h. das Märchen entfaltet nicht mehr ungehemmt seine Wirkung als »enchantment«, worin Riten und Grenzüberschreitungen (Pubertät, Defloration) mit identitätsstiftender Funktion aufgehoben werden. Vielmehr wird in erster Linie der Intellekt des Lesers angesprochen. Das zeigt sich zum Teil an den lexikalischen Besonderheiten: Der Text enthält eine Anzahl seltener englischer und fremdsprachlicher Vokabeln und verwendet sowohl Wissenschaftssprache als auch archaisierendes Englisch. Viele Elemente aus der umgangssprachlichen Lexik unterlaufen jedoch diese Wirkung wieder.

Inhaltlich wird das Amalgamieren heterogener Elemente durch die Erwähnung der Sexualität – vor allem der großen Genitalien des Wolfsmenschen – und durch – ebenfalls märchenuntypische – religiöse Requisiten wie z. B. die Bibel oder den zeitlichen Rahmen des Weihnachtsfestes betont.

Die Überdeterminiertheit erweist sich vielleicht besonders deutlich am Beispiel der Farbe Rot, die ja dem Ursprungstext und seiner Protagonistin den Namen gab. Mehrfach betont der neue Text, dass Rot – für das hier ein scharlachroter Umhang steht – die Farbe des Blutes ist: des Opferblutes, des Menstruationsblutes, des Blutstropfens bei der Defloration, des Klatschmohns, der auf den Schlachtfeldern blüht, des Blutstropfens im Märchen »Schneewittchen«. Diese Assoziationen werden in der Short Story determinatorisch festgelegt, sie sind nicht mehr frei assoziierbar. Dennoch enthält auch sie Passagen mit magischer Wirkung: Das metonymische weiße Haarbüschel der getöteten Großmutter im Kaminfeuer löst bei Rotkäppchen Todesangst aus; »the blood she must spill« assoziiert zunächst ihren Tod, meint aber die Defloration – eine Art kleiner Tod, eine irreversible Veränderung. Das Ver-

brennen der Kleider symbolisiert ebenfalls diese Station des Abschiednehmens und Grenzüberschreitens.
Dennoch zeigt sich auch hier die Wechselwirkung von Magie und (Um-)Deutung: Walpurgisnacht, Drudenfuß und Wintersonnenwende auf der einen Seite, christliches Weihnachtsfest und Exorzismen auf der anderen; Grenzlinien verschwimmen, auch die zwischen Mensch und Tier.
Die Magie von Carters Erzählung wird intensiviert durch die Verbindung von Ewiggültigem (»always«) und sowohl räumlich als auch zeitlich Spezifiziertem (»in our village, Christmas Eve«); sprachlich wird diese Wirkung durch die Verwendung der Tempora erzielt: »Simple present« und »simple past« wechseln einander ab und werden zu einem ewigen »Immer«, »a hugely extended Now« (John Fowles), in dem Vergangenheit, Gegenwart und Zukunft verschwimmen und die lineare Zeitvorstellung irrelevant wird.
Wie wirkt nun ein so komplexer und kunstvoll erzählter Text? Zunächst mag der interpretierende Textanteil den Leser befremden; hier begegnet ihm ein verfremdetes Märchen, das (s)eine Interpretation bereits enthält, darüber hinaus aber auch zahlreiche andere Textquellen benutzt. Es irritiert und regt zur Auseinandersetzung mit den intellektualisierenden wie den emotiven Strategien an. »Stimmt« die psychoanalytische Interpretation, oder ist sie wenigstens plausibel? Wie erklärt sich das kannibalistische Motiv? Anders als im zweiten Textbeispiel von Emma Tennant wird hier nicht die nachfolgende, sondern die vorausgehende Generation verschlungen. Was hat es mit den Elementen der christlichen Religion auf sich? Welchen Zweck erfüllen die wie sprachliche Versatzstücke eingestreuten Definitionen und Beschreibungen (vgl. etwa »the robin, the friend of man, sits on the handle of the gardener's spade and sings«, S. 43)? Welche Erzählperspektive liegt zugrunde? Die Polyvalenz von Texten und Interpretationen wird zum Thema in Carters Geschichte. Sie enthüllt hyperbolisch den intertextuellen Charakter von Literatur: Jedem neuen Text gehen literarische und nichtliterarische Texte

voran, präformierend, suggestiv, assoziierend. Kreativ ist die Zusammensetzung zu einem »neuen« Textgebilde, einem Text-Patchwork über den Wolf – oder doch über den Menschen?

Fay Weldon, »In the Great War« (1985)

Die Autorin ist sowohl für ihre satirischen Fähigkeiten und feministischen Aussagen als auch für ihre Feminismuskritik bekannt. In ihren Romanen und Short Stories variiert sie häufig das Thema des Verhältnisses von Frauen zu anderen Frauen.
Der im Titel der vorliegenden Erzählung genannte Krieg erhält gleich zu Beginn eine neue Bedeutung. In Großbritannien meint man mit »Great War« im allgemeinen den Ersten Weltkrieg. Die Erzählerfigur funktioniert diese Bedeutung jedoch um in den während der fünfziger Jahre stattfindenden Krieg der Frauen um einen Mann und fügt hinzu, dass sich »heute« – vermutlich als Folge der Emanzipationswelle der siebziger Jahre – die Frauen zu einem »neuen Krieg«, »a cold war« (S. 80), zusammengeschlossen hätten: dem Kampf gegen die Männer.
Das Thema weiblicher Rivalität um einen Mann als Versorger und Ernährer wird direkt, ohne Umschweife und Euphemismen oder Einhaltung von Tabus behandelt. Die für Weldon charakteristische Fragmentarisierung des Erzählens führt zu einer Vielzahl kurzer und kürzester Abschnitte, die parallele, einander spiegelnde und sich überkreuzende Erzählstränge ermöglicht. Die auktoriale Erzählperspektive folgt meist einer der weiblichen Figuren und schenkt den Frauen die Hauptaufmerksamkeit. Dabei werden die Männer aber nicht aus den Augen verloren; ihre Darstellung ist an Komik mindestens so reich wie die ihrer Partnerinnen.
Mehrere Generationen folgen aufeinander – eine Seltenheit in der Gattung Short Story – und verkörpern so auch einen Teil der Zeitgeschichte: Patty repräsentiert die ›gute‹ Ehefrau der

fünfziger Jahre, deren Ehemann Arthur ihr von einer Rivalin, Helene, ausgespannt wird. Mit anders verteilten Rollen wiederholt sich dasselbe Spiel: Pattys und Arthurs Tochter Enid dringt in die Ehe von Walter Walther ein, der seine Frau Rosanne daraufhin verlässt und Enid heiratet, später aber die schwangere Enid und seine Töchter aus erster Ehe, die mittlerweile zu ihm und Enid gezogen sind, verlässt, um zu seiner ersten Ehefrau zurückzukehren.

Dieses repetitive Handlungs- und Personenkonstellationsmuster drückt im Wandel das stets Gleiche aus. Frauen führen Krieg gegen andere Frauen, gewinnen und verlieren, können entweder ihre Waffen gebrauchen oder sind selbst schuld, wenn sie dabei versagen. Gelegentlich wirkt dieser »Krieg« etwas retrospektiv und scheint in erster Linie Elemente des Frauenbildes der fünfziger und sechziger Jahre bis 1968 widerzuspiegeln: Ablehnung des Intellekts in Frauen, patriarchalische Familienmuster, Raffinesse als Hauptwaffe der Frauen, die Ehe als sicheres Plätzchen fern von der Welt des Geldverdienens. Rollentrennung und Aufgabenverteilung, der Verlust des Ehemannes an eine Jüngere – alle Klischees der Frauenromane dieser Epoche werden heraufbeschworen und erweisen sich als unschlagbar. Auch vor Zynismus schreckt Weldon nicht zurück: Scheinheiligkeit, Verstellung, Intrigen werden hier als typisch weiblich dargestellt, und trotz der vorhandenen Abhängigkeit der Frauen von den Männern sind diese die Dummen. Die Frauen selbst stützen sogar die patriarchalische Rollenverteilung – und zwar so lange, bis sich Attraktivität, Fügsamkeit und Perfektionierung der hausfraulichen Fähigkeiten als wirkungslos erweisen, während früher die Kausalität zwischen weiblichem Unvermögen und Scheitern der Ehe zwingend erschien. Enid streckt die Waffen, als ihr Kind geboren wird, gibt den Krieg auf und lebt in einer Art weiblicher Kommune (der späten siebziger Jahre) mit ihren fast gleichaltrigen Stieftöchtern und ihrer kleinen Tochter Belinda – der Mann kehrt zu seiner ersten Frau zurück. Die Zukunft ist weiblich, die Fronten verlaufen anders.

Fay Weldons wirkungsvollste Erzählpassagen finden sich in der Aufdeckung psychischer und gesellschaftlicher Mechanismen. Ihre erbarmungslose, aber auch abgeklärte Scharfzüngigkeit ist oft ein Stein des Anstoßes. Die nachhaltige Wirkung resultiert weiterhin aus der Analogie zwischen Fragmentarisierung des Erzählstroms und Episodenhaftigkeit der zwischenmenschlichen Beziehungen: Nichts ist von Dauer, Konstellationen wechseln ständig, auch aufrichtige Gefühle erweisen sich als trügerisch.
»Gender« ist das explizite und implizite Thema der Short Story: Männer und Frauen zeigen kulturell bedingte Wesensmerkmale, die wandelbar sind und auch das Verhältnis der Geschlechter zueinander einem ständigen Wandel unterwerfen. Nur die Veränderung ist von Dauer.

Sara Maitland, »The Wicked Stepmother's Tale« (1987)

Diese Short Story ist ein weiteres Beispiel für die Neufassung eines Märchens; darin liefert sie einen Kontrastvergleich zu Emma Tennants »Philomela« und Angela Carters »The Company of Wolves«.
Der Anfang des Märchentextes von »Aschenputtel« bildet die Folie, von deren Hintergrund sich die neue Version abhebt. Die Variante stellt eine Werteumkehrung durch monoperspektivisches Erzählen dar. Die böse Stiefmutter gibt eine »Gegendarstellung« zum Volksmärchen ab, in der Aschenputtel als liebes, aber einfältiges Geschöpf erscheint, dessen Verhalten keineswegs belohnt wird. Als Ich-Erzählerin vermag die Stiefmutter dem Leser ausführlich ihre Sicht darzulegen. Ihre Argumente gründen sich hauptsächlich auf Populärpsychologie: Aschenputtel, deren Lebenslauf sich in dieser Geschichte ja nicht mehr zum Guten wendet, ist lebensuntüchtig, allzu duldsam und sanft; dadurch provoziert sie ihre Stiefmutter, sie zu kritisieren und später vor allem seelisch grausam zu quälen.
Die Motive der Stiefmutter stehen im Vordergrund. Ihr Zorn

auf die »infantile« Stieftochter, die nicht hart und kalt genug ist und ihre Ellbogen nicht gebrauchen kann, zeugt selbst von seelischen Problemen. Es ist eine Geschichte von »victim« und »victimiser«, wobei auch die Stiefmutter Opfer einer Behandlung ist, welche auf seelische Bedürfnisse nur unzureichend Rücksicht nimmt. Die Short Story setzt sich jedoch vor allem mit einem Frauenbild auseinander, das seit dem 18. Jahrhundert dominiert: mit der jungen Frau, deren widerspruchsloses, passives und demütiges Wesen hier als Ergebnis einer Verformung erscheint und sie »unfit for life« macht.
Insofern wird Bilderstürmerei betrieben. Darüber hinaus werden die märchentypischen starren Grenzlinien zwischen Gut und Böse unterlaufen. Dennoch ergibt sich keine Neubewertung. Im schnodderigen, Wortwahl und Syntax der Umgangssprache aufgreifenden Erzählstil drückt sich nicht nur die Attitüde einer Ellbogengesellschaft aus, sondern auch ein Mangel an Sensibilität bei der Erzählerin und die Tendenz zu einer neuen Art von Vereinfachung, die aber lediglich eine klischeehafte Verkehrung von Hauptaspekten des Ursprungstextes ins Gegenteil bewirkt. Statt der Einfachheit des Volksmärchens zeigt sich hier ein Mangel an Differenziertheit. Das komplexe Thema seelischer Verletzungen kann kaum durch eine monologische Erzählsituation und platte Umkehrungstechnik angemessen dargestellt werden. Darin steckt allerdings auch eine Provokation an die Adresse des Lesers, der sich einer Reaktion nicht mehr erwehren kann. Sympathisch wird ihm die Hauptfigur der Erzählung wohl kaum werden; doch immerhin kommt die im Märchen stumme Stiefmutter hier zu Wort, und siehe da: sie hat etwas zu sagen! Das umfassendere Thema der »stummen Frauen«, deren Nicht-zu-Wort-Kommen schließlich durchbrochen wird, weist auch auf den konservativ-patriarchalischen Grundzug des Volksmärchens hin. Die identitätsstiftende Rolle des Sprechens und Sich-Artikulierens stellt diese Short Story thematisch daher in die Gruppe der auf feministischer Tradition basierenden Erzählungen: Zumindest ansatzweise werden Aschenputtel und ihre Stiefmutter aus

Rollenzwängen nicht nur des Märchens, sondern auch überkommener Vorstellungen von Weiblichkeit befreit. Zugleich werden aber neue, modernere Klischees verbreitet: dass die Welt angeblich dem Rücksichtslosen gehört und dass die Realität rational erklärbar ist. Ich betrachte dies trotz der subversiven Ansätze eher als eine affirmative Haltung gegenüber der »objektiven« Wirklichkeit, als mimetisches Erzählen und als Fortsetzung eines männlichen Sprachgebrauchs im Diskurs der Erklärung.

Penelope Fitzgerald, »At Hiruharama« (1992)

Dies ist nur zum Schein eine einfache Short Story, leicht zu lesen, ohne narrative Zugangsschwierigkeiten oder komplizierte Handlungen und Charaktere. Vielmehr handelt es sich um einen komplexen Text, der viele Themen und Aussagen beinhaltet: die Situation der Kolonisten, verschiedene Frauenbilder aus männlicher Sicht, Einsamkeit, Schwangerschaft, Geburt, eurozentrische Vorstellungen über Ehe, Elternschaft und Fortschritt. Das Geschehen wird aus der Perspektive eines Enkels erzählt, dessen trockener Humor die Charaktere einfältig und simpel erscheinen lässt. Das Element von Verschmitztheit und Ironie mildert die Härte des geschilderten Kolonistenlebens und den Bruch mit einer Reihe von Tabus, die insbesondere Zeugung, Schwangerschaft und Geburt sowie generell die wechselseitige Abhängigkeit von Mann und Frau umgeben.
Die Erzählung spielt im neuseeländischen *back country* und ist eine neue, umgedrehte Version der *Genesis*: Die Erde muss urbar gemacht werden, der Mann eine Gefährtin bekommen, und die Menschheit muss sich vermehren. Das Ur-Paar Tanner und Kitty kommt aus der Zivilisation in die Wildnis, und zwar schrittweise: aus England nach Auckland, von da nach Awanui und weiter ins Hinterland. Das absolute Pionierdasein wird von dem Junggesellen wider Willen Brinkman (dessen Name umschrieben werden könnte als »the man

who lives on the brink [of humanity and civilization]«) verkörpert.

Die beiden Protagonisten handeln gemäß dem biblischen Auftrag »Macht euch die Erde untertan« sowie »Seid fruchtbar und mehret euch«. Die religiöse Überzeugung erweist sich jedoch als unzureichend, da sie nicht im Paradies leben (obgleich der werdende Vater glaubt, Hiruharama bedeute »Jerusalem«, S. 96), sondern an der *frontier*, der Zivilisationsgrenze, die im 18. und frühen 19. Jahrhundert eine prägende Rolle in der nordamerikanischen Geistesgeschichte und Literatur spielte. Für Neuseeland gilt dies auch im frühen 20. Jahrhundert. Doch anders als in Nordamerika gibt es hier ein friedvolles Nebeneinander von Maori-Bevölkerung und europäischen Kolonisten, auch wenn die Einheimischen oft als Diener der Einwanderer arbeiten.

Das Hauptaugenmerk soll bei dieser Short Story allerdings der feministischen Komponente gelten. Dass die Zukunft weiblich ist, geht als Botschaft von ihr aus. Dem zivilisationsgewohnten Leser mag der Verlauf der geschilderten Familiengründung absurd erscheinen: ein Leben in der Wildnis, anstelle ärztlicher Versorgung einige wohlgemeinte Ratschläge, statt Telefon Brieftauben, statt der Hebamme bei der Geburt ein hilfloser Ehemann.

Die Geburt ist – obgleich »objektiv« recht komplikationslos – ein Naturereignis von archaischer und fast brutaler Monumentalität. Kitty, die Stellvertreterin der Zivilisation, ist bis zur Geburt ihrer Zwillingstöchter die einzige Frau weit und breit. Auch in den Wehen ist sie noch um Konversation bemüht und schenkt der Ankunft des Nachbarn Brinkman und seiner Bewirtung Aufmerksamkeit. Doch kann man sie nicht als »round character« dieser Erzählung apostrophieren; sie bleibt noch schablonenhafter als die männlichen Figuren. Trotz des primär »weiblichen« Themas gibt es keine weibliche Perspektive: Denken und Fühlen Kittys bleiben fast völlig ausgeklammert. Als markanteste, heterogene Merkmale treten ihre Bildungsansprüche – Bedingung für ihre Heirat mit

Tanner war, dass er zuvor Lesen und Schreiben erlernt – und ihre Schmerzen und lauten Schreie während der Geburt ohne ärztlichen Beistand hervor. Mit ihrer biologischen Rolle und ihrer humorvoll dargestellten Zukunftsorientiertheit verkörpert diese Frau Natur u n d Kultur. Es dominiert zwar die männliche Perspektive, doch die Männer agieren bei dem zentralen Ereignis der Geschichte nur als ungeschicktes Hilfspersonal, und wären nicht die Brieftauben gewesen, wer weiß, ob dann der zweite Säugling, die später erfolgreiche Rechtsanwältin, überhaupt hätte gerettet werden können!
»Hiruharama is not Paradise«, muss man sagen, doch scheint sich dort für die kurze Erzählzeit die Keimzelle der Menschheit zu befinden. Der sachliche Erzählstil – parataktisch, lexikalisch von holzschnittartiger Einfachheit, mit wortkargen Charakteren – vermittelt ein Ereignis von urtümlicher, auch ergreifender Simplizität und ungeahnter Tragweite: Frauenüberschuss in einer männlich dominierten und doch – oder gerade deswegen – defizitären Gesellschaft.

Nadine Gordimer, »Homage« (1995)

Die vorliegende Erzählung, eine Short Short Story der Nobelpreisträgerin, benutzt das Prinzip der Reduktion und Verneinung: Kommunikation, Identität, Sinn, Differenz und auch Humanität werden verneint oder minimalisiert.
In seinem stummen Selbstgespräch gibt der Ich-Erzähler dem Leser, der von Anfang an die Rolle des Gegenübers in der U-Bahn einnimmt, Rätsel auf: Exposition und deiktische Hinweise fehlen, so dass trotz der unkomplizierten Erzählsituation die Zuordnung erschwert wird; die verwendeten Possessiv- und Personalpronomen geben keinen Aufschluss, sondern erhalten die Anonymität aufrecht. Diese, so erkennt der Leser, ist notwendig für den Ich-Erzähler, weil er ein vom organisierten Verbrechen angeheuerter Killer ist, der einen Mann, der Bedeutung und Ruhm im öffentlichen Leben genoss, getötet hat. Aber auch das Opfer und andere Personen – Auftrag-

geber, Passanten, die Frau des Ermordeten – bleiben anonym und schemenhaft. Das Puzzle, aus dem der Leser bruchstückhaft Informationen zusammensetzt, bleibt ein Fragment, und keine der Figuren erhält Gesicht, erkennbare Stimme, Aussehen oder Eigenschaften. Die ungelösten Rätsel weisen nicht auf dringliche Fragen; Indifferenz liegt über dem ganzen Geschehen, und die Identität des Killers bleibt verschleiert. Auch seine Sichtweise teilt sich dem Leser nur bruchstückhaft mit. Grenzen werden überschritten und annulliert, ohne dass dies den Ich-Erzähler zu berühren scheint. Seine Gefühlswelt bleibt ebenfalls weitgehend »auf Null« reduziert; bildlich gesprochen hat er sich selbst mit seinem Opfer eliminiert. Dem trägt der Schlusssatz Rechnung: Der Name des Täters – und damit seine Identität – sind mit dem Opfer seiner Tat begraben; sie existieren nicht, weil niemand sie kennt. Trotz verschiedener Gelegenheitsjobs bleibt der Täter ein Fremder für alle, nicht nur für den Leser: »I don't take up with anybody. Not even a woman« (S. 110). Er kann am leichtesten untertauchen, indem er das tut, was alle tun: auf das Grab seines Opfers Blumen legen.

So erweist sich die Ehrerbietung, die er dem Toten zollt, als ironische, ja zynische Geste, die dem Schutz des Täters vor Ergreifung dienen soll. Die Ironie wird unterstrichen durch die mangelnde Sorgfalt bei der Auswahl der Blumen und die geringen Kosten für den Strauß.

Ist die Erzählung mehr als eine vordergründige Kriminalgeschichte, ein Politthriller im Kleinformat? Der Killer als Metapher des Individuums in einer Gesellschaft der (Selbst-)Entfremdung und Kommunikationslosigkeit – erscheint diese Interpretation zu gewagt? Der Text verweigert Bedeutung, obwohl seine Lektüre keineswegs schwierig ist. Eine kafkaeske Situation mit dem Täter als Opfer – Opfer von Anonymität, Irrelevanz moralischer Kategorien und Auslöschung aller Grenzen, ohne kausalen Zusammenhang, ohne Konsequenzen, ohne Ende. Die Frage nach dem Sinn stellt sich kaum; die Deutung bleibt dem Leser überlassen.

Rose Tremain, »The Beauty of the Dawn Shift« (1996)

Die Autorin wurde durch ihren historiographischen Roman *Restoration* (1989), der in den sechziger Jahren des 17. Jahrhunderts spielt, bekannt. Auch in ihren Short Stories ist die Neufassung der Geschichte ein sehr wichtiges Thema. In »The Beauty of the Dawn Shift« behandelt sie eine noch nicht lange zurückliegende Zeit der deutschen Geschichte: die »Wende« von 1989/90. Dass dies durch eine Britin geschieht und dazu nur etwa fünf Jahre nach den realen Ereignissen, ist an sich schon bemerkenswert. Überrascht, vielleicht auch befremdet, wird der Leser jedoch über die revisionistische Geschichtsschreibung sein, die in der Short Story zutage tritt.
Aufgrund der Kombination von auktorialer und personaler Erzählsituation hängt die Sichtweise der historisch bedeutsamen Zäsur wesentlich von der Reflektorfigur ab. Hector S., ein Ostberliner, ist aber trotz seines martialischen Namens und seiner Tätigkeit als Grenzsoldat in der NVA eine klägliche Gestalt, und zwar in psychischer, sozialer und intellektueller Hinsicht – jemand, auf den keine politische Richtung oder Staatsform besonders stolz sein kann. Hector hat sein Leben geographisch und geistig in der DDR verbracht, er entstammt einer unglücklichen Familie, in der lediglich das inzestuöse Verhältnis zu seiner Schwester eine Quelle der Freude für ihn darstellte. Jetzt, nach Öffnung der Mauer und angesichts des bevorstehenden Endes der DDR, entschließt sich Hector, nach Osten zu gehen, dorthin, wo er glaubt, noch Anhänger seines geistigen Zuhauses, des real existierenden Sozialismus, finden zu können. Die Grenzen, die ihn umgeben, bleiben erhalten, weil nur sie seine Identität sichern. Deshalb kann er die »Wende« nicht freudig begrüßen, sondern versucht vergeblich, seine verlorengegangene »Autorität« als NVA-Grenzposten aufrechtzuerhalten, und sei es, um den Diebstahl von Blumenzwiebeln auf dem Friedhof zu verhindern.
Das Schäbige und Kleinbürgerliche seiner Umgebung stört den Protagonisten nicht; der Leser nimmt es durch den aukto-

rialen Erzähler wahr, ebenso wie die Verwendung von auktorialer und personaler Erzählsituation ihm die morbide Absurdität der Charaktere offenbart. Für Hector ist der real existierende Sozialismus Heimat; nicht aus fester politischer Überzeugung etwa, sondern weil dies die einzige Wirklichkeit ist, die er kennt, will er dorthin, wo er glaubt, den Marxismus noch in einem kommunistisch regierten Staat vorzufinden.

Die Reise nach Osten endet zunächst in Polen, wo er auch der (gesamt)deutschen Vergangenheit begegnet, nämlich in Gestalt eines alten Bauernehepaares. Der alte Mann pflegt ihn während seiner Krankheit, aber die alte Frau lehnt ihn ab, weil er ein Deutscher in Uniform ist – das weckt zu viele schlechte Erinnerungen.

Die Zukunft scheint im Osten zu liegen; böswillig könnte man mit Ironie unterstellen, dieser NVA-Soldat suche neuen Lebensraum im Osten. Tatsächlich lauert dort eher die Vergangenheit, und zwar auch die noch vor dem Sozialismus liegende deutsche Vergangenheit. Hector fährt in einem Güterzug nach Osten, »cold as death«, und er fährt in seinen Tod. Die Verantwortung dafür wird von den Polen den Russen aufgebürdet – der Tote ist nur noch ein Relikt, das möglichst spurlos verschwinden muss.

Der physische Tod, der nicht ein gewaltsamer, sondern ein Tod durch Kälte ist, versinnbildlicht einen vorausgegangenen seelischen und sozialen Tod. Hector ist nichts mehr, und es wird klar, dass er niemals etwas war: was er vertrat, hat sich in Nichts aufgelöst; zudem war er auch ein klägliches NVA-Mitglied. Die Umwertung der Werte, »the somersault of history« (Graham Swift über die Französische Revolution), hat er weder gewollt noch bekämpft, auch nicht begrüßt, gefeiert oder genossen, zumal die Befreiung sich hauptsächlich als Konsumzwang zeigt (S. 117). Dies ist Geschichtsdarstellung aus der *loser*-Perspektive, aus dem Blickwinkel nicht nur einer Randfigur, sondern einer unterlegenen, ja, erbärmlichen Gestalt. Das Ende der Identität setzte allerdings schon ein, bevor das politische System zusammenbrach, das ihr scheinbar Stabilität verlieh. Der Protagonist ist ein Mensch, den Kärglichkeit und Authentizitätsmangel geprägt haben, der ohnmächtig und hilflos dem geschichtlichen Wandel ausgesetzt ist, bei dem er immer »unten« gewesen ist, ausgeliefert und nur zur Staffage mit Macht ausgestattet, instrumentalisiert und dann eliminiert.

Die »Lichtblicke« in dieser tristen und perspektivlosen Welt sind pastorale und ab und an sexuelle Bilder, die etwas »Schönes« verkörpern sollen, aber grotesk oder morbid wirken: der Schwan als Haustier in der Plattenbausiedlung, später gespiegelt in den mit Kranichen verglichenen Schwänen auf einem See, von denen Hector in seinem imaginären Brief an Ute erzählt; das Nacktfoto der Schwester, besonders aber die halluzinatorischen Vorstellungen von der Landschaft und unverdorbenen Natur. Die Short Story ist der Bericht von einer Reise in ein fernes Land, die entgegen üblichen Vorstellungen nicht ins Unbekannte, sondern ins Vertraute (zurück)führen soll, weg aus dem Ungewissen, wo Hector eine Null geworden ist, ins Schöne, Ehrenhafte, »Anständige«, Bekannte. Das einzig Gewisse aber ist der Tod, der schon von Beginn der Erzählung an ein zentrales Thema war, ein Tod jedoch ohne jedes Pathos.

Das Zur-Sprache-Bringen von Tabus wird auch in dieser Geschichte Thema, und zwar nicht nur am Beispiel eines tabuisierten sexuellen Verhaltens (Inzest), sondern auch im Hinblick auf Hoffnungslosigkeit, Glanzlosigkeit und Elend eines geschichtsträchtigen Moments. Der Winter 1989/90 wurde – so macht die Erzählung deutlich – nicht von allen Menschen mit Euphorie, Enthusiasmus und Freiheitstaumel erlebt. Hector ist einer von denen, die damals alles einbüßten und keine Perspektive mehr besaßen, außer vielleicht in der Fantasie.[3] Er ist aber auch kein zukünftiger Linker oder PDSler, auch kein Durchschnittsmensch, sondern gehört, wie der Verlauf der

3 Der Roman *Die Blechtrommel* (1959) von Günter Grass bildet eine Analogie.

Short Story verdeutlicht, ins Abseits der Gesellschaft: eine peinliche Figur.

Geschichte, so sagt heute ein Gemeinplatz, wird monoperspektivisch von der jeweils herrschenden Gruppe geschrieben – und wieder umgeschrieben. Zu ihr gehörte Hector nie – wie sein Vater sarkastisch zu Beginn unter Anspielung auf das Märchen vom Froschkönig andeutete –, weder vor noch nach der Wende, die hier weder eine zum Besseren noch wirklich zum Schlechteren ist. Er bleibt ohne Wirkung, ohne Individualität, ohne Glück, ohne Auftrag. Hier gibt es kein »Wehe den Besiegten!« – Hecti war immer schon *loser*. Dies ist Geschichte aus der Sicht einer Null, der am Ende gar noch die Sympathie des Lesers versagt bleiben mag, der betreten schnell weiterliest. Die ironische Brechung, die der Wechsel zwischen auktorialer und personaler Erzählperspektive entstehen lässt, gibt einen Durchblick auf die erbärmliche Kleinheit eines großen Augenblicks frei. Dieses Tabu zu brechen, ist der Autorin gelungen, und der Leser reagiert mit Verlegenheit auf die Enthüllung.

Kathy Page, »It is July, Now« (1996)

Die Autorin hat noch nicht den Bekanntheitsgrad der meisten anderen in diesem Band vertretenen Schriftstellerinnen erlangt. Ihre Short Story ist gleichwohl thematisch von großer Aktualität: Zwei Welten, Ost und West, prallen zusammen in Gestalt von zwei Frauen. Gleichzeitig ist es die einzige der vorliegenden Short Stories, die im Universitätsmilieu spielt.

Die Ich-Erzählerin ist Dozentin an einer Universität in einem der baltischen Staaten, vermutlich Estland. Dies kann der Leser aus zahlreichen Details schließen: Das Land wurde kürzlich »befreit«, es grenzt an die See, der Taxifahrer ist ein Russe, man kann finnische Fernsehsender empfangen (und wohl auch verstehen), die Landessprache ist weitgehend unbekannt und hat eine sehr komplizierte Grammatik (was wie die Eigennamen Piret und Kaarmanni Olletuba eine Zugehörigkeit zur finnisch-ugrischen Sprachgruppe nahelegt), es herrscht Mangel an vielen Dingen sowohl im Wissenschaftsbetrieb als auch im täglichen Leben, es ist sehr kalt. Eine Exposition fehlt jedoch.

Die zweite Hauptperson ist eine ausländische Gastdozentin, deren Betreuung die Protagonistin Piret, alleinerziehende Mutter einer fast erwachsenen Tochter namens Katrin, widerstrebend übernimmt. Ganz allmählich findet eine Annäherung der beiden Frauen statt, wobei die Ausländerin – Amerikanerin vermutlich – die Initiative übernimmt. Ihre Neugier und ihr Wissensdurst sind der misstrauisch-verschlossenen Ich-Erzählerin erst lästig, bis sie nach der Abreise der Gastdozentin bemerkt, dass auch sie selbst ein Bedürfnis hat, sich jemandem mitzuteilen, und zwar bemerkenswerterweise eher einer fremden Person, »someone from outside« (S. 162). Sie taut ganz langsam aus einer Art seelischem Permafrost auf und erzählt schließlich von ihrer Katze, ihren Essensgewohnheiten und von Blumenzwiebeln. In diesem Prozess keimen Erinnerungen an den Vater Katrins auf, und allmählich erwacht auch Pirets Interesse an ihrem Gegenüber; erst ganz kurz vor dem Ende fragt sie sich, wie alt die Andere wohl sein mag und ob sie eventuell verheiratet ist.

Trotz großer Disparatheit haben die drei Erzählungen der vorliegenden Sammlung, die im früheren Ostblock spielen (»The Beauty of the Dawn Shift«, eventuell »Homage« und »It is July, Now«), die Kargheit und Ärmlichkeit gemeinsam, durch die *setting* und Charaktere gekennzeichnet sind. Sie stellen das Erleben einer Mangelsituation aus unterschiedlichen Blickwinkeln in den Mittelpunkt, und in allen drei Short Stories wird die materielle Mangelsituation zur Metapher eines tieferen Mangels.

Neben Einsamkeit und Kommunikation sind die Not und Plackerei des täglichen Lebens im dargestellten Land Hauptgegenstand von »It is July, Now«. Das »Absterben« von innerem Leben, von Erinnerung und Kommunikationswunsch korreliert mit dem Kampf ums Überleben; die Besucherin

kennt diesen Kampf nicht und geht daher sorglos mit Kopierpapier, Geld und der Geduld ihrer Gastgeberin um, die mehr Geld für die tierärztliche Behandlung ihrer Katze als für ihren Lebensunterhalt ausgibt; trotzdem stirbt die Katze.
Die andersartige wirtschaftliche Situation im Gastland wirkt sich in allen Bereichen des Lebens aus. Die Short Story gibt eine Reihe von Szenen wieder, die dies verdeutlichen und so die Diskrepanz zwischen den beiden Frauen erkennbar werden lassen: Eine Einladung, der Wunsch zu telefonieren oder die Unterhaltung über persönliche Dinge stellen sämtlich Hürden dar, die zu überwinden Piret sich scheut. Kälte bekommt auch hier eine symbolische Bedeutung: Das Ich wirkt aber nicht nur wie erstarrt, sondern auch abweisend, wie gepanzert durch harte Lebenserfahrung. Dieser Panzer hilft Piret zwar zu überleben, das Notwendige zu tun und sich den Gegebenheiten anzupassen, macht sie aber auch wenig mitteilsam und lässt sie nach recht starren Regeln und Verhaltensmustern leben und handeln. Durch ihr persönliches Schicksal wird diese Prägung verstärkt: Vom Vater ihrer Tochter im Stich gelassen, empfindet sie gewiss Einsamkeit; paradoxerweise fühlt sie sich durch Andere aber auch schnell in ihrer Routine gestört. Die Besucherin ist ein Störenfried; »Störenfriede« im kargen Alltag sind außerdem die Tochter und die Katze, Pirets engste »Bezugspersonen«. Sie bringen aber auch eine heilsame Unruhe in ihr Leben, da Piret sich ihnen nicht verweigern kann und will, während sie der Gastdozentin zunächst nur das Nötigste an Gespräch, Interesse und Interaktion zu geben bereit ist. Die fremde Sprache stellt dabei noch ein zusätzliches Hindernis dar: Es kommt zwar einerseits zu Missverständnissen bei idiomatischen Redewendungen, aber dadurch werden andererseits Neugierde und Flexibilität gefördert. Schließlich erkennt Piret in der Situation der Besucherin, die kein Wort der Landessprache versteht, spiegelbildlich ein Stück weit sich selbst: »It must be like walking around with a shell around you which no one could get through, hard outside but very, very tender beneath« (S. 159).

Die Wandlung tritt ein, als sie, von der anderen Frau angesprochen, auf offener Straße zu weinen beginnt. Von da ab entsteht eine wärmere Atmosphäre; der Tod der Katze wird mit ihr, anders als im Gespräch mit Pirets Institutsdirektor, zu einem verbindenden Erlebnis, bei dem Verständnis und Austausch entstehen können. Piret empfindet schließlich so etwas wie Abschiedsschmerz, als sie den Gast zum Flughafen bringt. Dass sie die andere Frau vermisst, wird ihr erst klar, als diese nicht schreibt – sie vielleicht vergessen hat. Doch Pirets Lebensgefühl hat sich nachhaltig verändert; die Endlichkeit ist ihr bewusst geworden, und ihr Dasein ist weniger von Monotonie, mehr von Veränderung und neuer Erfahrung geprägt.

Antonia S. Byatt, »A Lamia in the Cevennes« (1996)

Einem ungewöhnlichen Titel folgt eine ungewöhnliche Geschichte, die Phantastisches und Wirkliches vermengt. Inmitten einer scheinbar mimetischen fiktiven Welt begegnen sowohl Protagonist als auch Leser der Erzählung von Imaginärem.

Die Lamia ist eigentlich ein Schreckenswesen, erotisch betörend und vernichtend, halb Mensch, halb Fisch, der Seejungfrau und der Fabel von der schönen Melusine verwandt. Schon im Titel wird die Kombination von Wirklichem – der reale Ort – und Imaginärem – das Fabelwesen – angedeutet. Im Unterschied zu etlichen anderen Short Stories steht hier eine Exposition am Anfang, die mit den wichtigsten Gegebenheiten vertraut macht: wer, wo, wann, warum?

Der Protagonist verläßt Thatcher-England, um in einer anderen Welt zu leben: mediterran, künstlerisch-offen, naturnah, sorglos, nicht-kommerzialisiert. Der Swimmingpool, den Bernard anlegen lässt, ist der Inbegriff dieser Werte und einer neugewonnenen Freiheit und Kreativität. Ein großer Teil der Darstellung gibt in auktorialer Erzählung das neue Lebensgefühl wieder, welches der Protagonist an dem neuen Handlungsort erlangt hat. Wetter, Licht, die Elemente sind ihm hier viel näher als andere Menschen. Doch gelingt es ihm nicht, in seiner Malerei künstlerisch zu verwirklichen, was ihm vorschwebt.

In diese ungestörte Idylle bricht das Übernatürliche plötzlich und unerwartet herein, zunächst als unerklärliche Verschmutzung, die vom Swimmingpool auf Bernard selbst übergreift und ihn in eine tiefe Krise stürzt: »I am polluted, my work is polluted, *I cannot go on*« (S. 172). Zwar finden die Schwimmbadbauer eine Erklärung, doch für Bernard bricht eine Welt zusammen. Nach Behebung dieser Störung tritt eine neue auf, die sich in Anrufen aus London äußert, der Welt, die er verlassen hat. Schließlich ist ein anderes Wesen, dessen Natur Bernard nicht erahnen kann, bei ihm eingedrungen und hat sich in dem gereinigten und neugefüllten Swimmingpool niedergelassen. Ein schlangenartiges Geschöpf gibt sich zu erkennen, allerdings nicht als männermordendes Schreckgespenst, sondern als erlösungsbedürftige, verwunschene Seejungfrau mit romantischen Vorstellungen: »And then you will kiss me, and we will be married, and I shall have an immortal soul?« (S. 183). Bernard aber will sie lediglich malen, weitere Sympathien hegt er nicht für sie, trotz all ihrer Bemühungen. Der Künstler kennt nur seine Kunst; der Wunsch der Lamia, von ihm in eine Frau verwandelt zu werden, verhallt ungehört. Die Ankunft seines Freundes Raymond führt auf unsanfte Weise ins wirkliche Leben zurück und bedeutet auch das Verschwinden der Lamia: Raymond bringt als seine Gefährtin eine junge, sexuell aufreizende Frau mit Namen Melanie (›die Schwarze‹) mit. Ist der Name ein Anklang an Melusine? Ist Melanie die Lamia? Explizit wird dies nicht bestätigt, doch kommt der Leser gemeinsam mit Bernard zu diesem Schluss. Die Ironie der Verwandlung liegt in ihrer Inadäquatheit: Der Künstler konnte sich das Fantasiewesen nicht anverwandeln, sondern fand es durch die Übertragung in andere Kunstformen vermittelt. Vor allem John Keats' Gedicht »Lamia« zeigt ihm ein trügerisches Bild, voll dunkler Mächte und Gefahren, das Dämonische im Eros, erinnert ihn aber auch an die beschränkte Weltsicht des naturwissenschaftlichen Denkens, das die Faszination des Künstlers für die Geheimnisse seiner Erlebniswelt nicht zu erfassen vermag. Die Lamia wird nicht etwa Bernards Muse, sondern seine Obsession: »They were each other's prisoners, he and she« (S. 185). Sein Freund aber erhält ein »girl-friend« vom Typ Femme fatale in einem trivialeren Sinn: ein wenig schrill, ein bißchen zu sexy, keine »immortal soul«, nichts für den Künstler Bernard. Er bleibt allein zurück und wird glücklich in seiner Malerei. Die Lamia entpuppt sich als ein proteisches Wesen: Für jeden bedeutet sie etwas Anderes.

In gewissem Sinn stellt die Verwandlung der Lamia ein Gegenstück zu Angela Carters Werwolf-Geschichte dar, mit der sie auch den mythischen Ursprung gemeinsam hat. Antonia S. Byatts modernes Märchen verwendet spielerische Ironie und flicht eine ganze Reihe von Themen und Stilelementen ein, die zu einer Postmodernisierung der Erzählprosa beitragen, wie etwa die Intertextualität, nicht nur in markierten, als Zitate kenntlich gemachten Textstellen von Keats, sondern auch in nicht-markierten Zitaten und Anspielungen wie etwa »the bliss of solitude« (Wordsworth), »your wits are turning« (Shakespeare). Ferner thematisiert es den Dialog der Künste (Malerei, Dichtung), die Pluralität des Lebens einzelner Menschen (Raymond und Bernard studierten zusammen »theatre design« an der Kunsthochschule; einer wurde Szenenbildner für eine Kinder-Fernsehserie, der andere ein esoterischer Maler, der Matisse nacheifert), die Aneignung eines Fabelwesens in unterschiedlichen Frauenbildern, ein Sprachen-Babylon (nicht zufällig haben die Figuren Namen, die englisch oder französisch ausgesprochen werden können), die Metamorphose und nicht zuletzt auch das grenzauflösende Medium von Wasser, Licht und Farbe.

So bündeln sich eine große Anzahl verschiedener Themen in der scheinbar mimetischen Erzählung, in der das Fantastische einen subversiven Effekt erzielt: Das Bild der Wirklichkeit löst sich auf in Bildern.

Barbara Puschmann-Nalenz

Fremdsprachentexte

IN RECLAMS UNIVERSAL-BIBLIOTHEK

Englische und amerikanische Dramen

Samuel Beckett: Waiting for Godot. 147 S. UB 9214

Brendan Behan: The Hostage. 141 S. UB 9222

Five English Short Plays. Brenton, Bond, Stoppard, Pinter, Churchill. 210 S. UB 9062

Hanif Kureishi: My Beautiful Laundrette. 166 S. UB 9063

Arthur Miller: The Crucible. 224 S. UB 9257 – Death of a Salesman. 171 S. UB 9172

Marc Norman / Tom Stoppard: Shakespeare in Love. 181 S. UB 9072

Eugene O'Neill: Long Day's Journey into Night. 216 S. UB 9252

J. B. Priestley: An Inspector Calls. 117 S. UB 9218

Willy Russell: Educating Rita. 132 S. UB 9040 – Shirley Valentine. 79 S. UB 9071

Peter Shaffer: Amadeus. 199 S. UB 9219

William Shakespeare: Hamlet. 261 S. UB 9292 – Macbeth. 167 S. UB 9220 – The Merchant of Venice 184 S. UB 9050 – A Midsummer Night's Dream. 160 S. UB 9247 – Romeo and Juliet. 219 S. UB 9005

Bernard Shaw: Mrs Warren's Profession. 198 S. UB 9166 – Pygmalion. 197 S. UB 9266

Tom Stoppard: Rosencrantz and Guildenstern are Dead. 171 S. UB 9185

John Millington Synge: The Playboy of the Western World. 128 S. UB 9211

Oscar Wilde: The Importance of Being Earnest. 141 S. UB 9267 – Lady Windermere's Fan. 101 S. UB 9187

Thornton Wilder: Our Town. 127 S. UB 9168

Tennessee Williams: Cat on a Hot Tin Roof. 224 S. UB 9039 – The Glass Menagerie. 149 S. UB 9178 – A Streetcar Named Desire. 199 S. UB 9240

Fremdsprachentexte

IN RECLAMS UNIVERSAL-BIBLIOTHEK

Short Stories · Auswahl

Afro-American Short Stories. Baldwin – Hughes – Jones – Kelley – Walker – Wright. 167 S. UB 9276

American Crime Stories. Cain – Collier – Ellin – MacDonald – Millar – Slesar. 167 S. UB 9268

American Film Stories. Boyle – Bradbury – Brautigan – Clark – Johnson – Johnston – Phillips – Saroyan – Shepard. 144 S. UB 9029

American Short Stories of the 19th Century. Bierce – Hawthorne – Irving – James – Melville – Poe – Twain. 300 S. UB 9034

Contemporary Australian Short Stories. Bail – Carey – Garner – Malouf – Moorhouse – Weller – White. 165 S. UB 9295

Contemporary American Short Stories. Barth – Barthelme – Godwin – Graham – Merwin – Oates – Pynchon – Updike – Vonnegut. 155 S. UB 9206

Contemporary Canadian Short Stories. Atwood – Findley – MacLeod – Munro – Richler – Valgardson – Wiebe. 189 S. UB 9261

Contemporary Irish Short Stories. Daly – Devlin – Friel – Healy – Kelly – Mac Mathúna – McGahern – Montague. 184 S. UB 9250

Contemporary New Zealand Short Stories. Frame – Gee – Grace – Hulme – Ihimaera – Stead. 168 S. UB 9035

Contemporary South African Short Stories. Bosman – Gordimer – Head – Hope – Matthews – Mphahlele – Roberts – Themba. 176 S. UB 9006

Detecting Woman. New American Short Stories. Dunlap – Grafton – Maron – McCafferty – McGrumb. 204 S. UB 9053

English Crime Stories. Allingham – Berkeley – Francis – James – Sayers. 165 S. UB 9254

English Love Stories. Bowen – Enright – Lawrence – Lessing – Lively – Mansfield – McEwan – O'Connor – Weldon. 174 S. UB 9047

Horror Stories of the Twentieth Century. Blackwood – Highsmith – King – Langley – Spark. 151 S. UB 9255

Many Voices – Many Cultures. Multicultural British Short Stories. Collins – Dabydeen – Dhondy – Gunesekera – Kureishi – O'Faolain – Rhys – Selvon – Shinebourne – Sinclair – Singh-Toor. 274 S. UB 9045

Modern American Short Stories. Anderson – Faulkner – Fitzgerald – Hemingway – Porter – Steinbeck. 160 S. UB 9216

Modern English Short Stories I. Bennett – de la Mare – Galsworthy – Hardy – Kipling – Maugham – Saki – Wells. 189 S. UB 9184

Modern English Short Stories II. Coppard – Forster – Graves – Greene – Hartley – Huxley – Lawrence – Pritchett – Waugh – Woolf. 184 S. UB 9165

Modern English Short Stories III. Amis – Bates – Lessing – McEwan – Sillitoe – Swift – Taylor – Wain – Wilson. 167 S. UB 9202

New York Fiction. Crane – Dreiser – O. Henry – Howe – Janowitz – Leacock – Marshall – Parker – Wolfe. 154 S. UB 9070

Science Fiction Stories I. Asimov – Ballard – Bester – De Graw – Dick. 152 S. UB 9156

Science Fiction Stories II. Ellison – Harrison – Heinlein – Russell – Wyndham. 191 S. UB 9210

Short Short Stories Universal. Thirty Stories from the English-speaking World. 229 S. UB 9297

Women's Fantastic Adventures. Le Guin – Moffett – Russ – Tiptree, Jr. 188 S. UB 9285

Philipp Reclam jun. Stuttgart